The
Little Catechism
of the
Curé of Ars

"And I will set up pastors over them,
and they shall feed them: they shall fear
no more, and they shall not be dis-
mayed: and none shall be wanting of
their number, saith the Lord."
—Jeremias 23:4

Lescuyer/Mappus

Saint John Marie Baptiste Vianney
The Curé of Ars
1786 - 1859
Patron Saint of Parish Priests

The
Little Catechism
of the
Curé of Ars

by

Saint John Vianney

Including

Instructions on the Catechism

and

Explanations and Exhortations

"And I will give you pastors according to my own heart, and they shall feed you with knowledge and doctrine."
—Jeremias 3:15

TAN BOOKS AND PUBLISHERS, INC.
Rockford, Illinois 61105

Nihil Obstat: Joseph D. Brokhage, S.T.D.
                 Censor Librorum

Imprimatur: ✠ Paul C. Schulte, D.D.
                 Archbishop of Indianapolis
                 April 6, 1951

The cover photograph is a picture of the statue sculpted by Cabuchet, a friend of the Curé of Ars. The statue can be seen at Ars in a shrine paid for by donations from the priests of France. Photograph: Editions Xavier Mappus, Lyon.

Library of Congress Catalog Card No.: 87-50943

ISBN: 0-89555-323-6

Printed and bound in the United States of America.

TAN BOOKS AND PUBLISHERS, INC.
P.O. Box 424
Rockford, Illinois 61105

1987

"And I will give you pastors according to my own heart, and they shall feed you with knowledge and doctrine."

—Jeremias 3:15

Contents

— Part I —
INSTRUCTIONS ON THE CATECHISM

— Part II —
EXPLANATIONS AND EXHORTATIONS

The Blessed Curé of Ars in His Catechetical Instructions

"THERE IS no doubt," says Père Gratry, "that, through purity of heart, innocence, either preserved or recovered by virtue, faith, and religion, there are in man capabilities and resources of mind, of body, and of heart which most people would not suspect. To this order of resources belongs what theology calls infused science, the intellectual virtues which the Divine Word inspires into our minds when He dwells in us by faith and love."

And Père Gratry quotes with enthusiasm, excusing himself for not translating them better, these magnificent words of a saint who lived in the eleventh century in one of the mystic monasteries on the banks of the Rhine: "This is what purifies the eye of the heart, and enables it to raise itself to the true light: contempt of worldly cares, mortification of the body, contrition of heart, abundance of tears...meditation on the admirable Essence of God and on His chaste Truth, fervent and pure prayer, joy in God, ardent desire for Heaven. Embrace all this," adds the saint, "and continue in it. Advance towards the light which offers itself to you as to its

sons, and descends of itself into your hearts. Take
your hearts out of your breasts, and give them
to Him who speaks to you, and He will fill them
with deific splendor, and you will be sons of light
and angels of God."

The description we have just read seems to have
been traced from the very life of the Curé of Ars.
Every detail recalls him, every feature harmonizes
marvelously with his. Who has ever carried further "contempt of worldly cares, mortification of
the body, abundance of tears?" He was always
bathed in tears. And then, "meditation on the
admirable Essence of God and on His chaste
Truth, and fervent and pure prayer, joy in God,
ardent desire for Heaven"—how characteristic is
this! "He had advanced towards the light, and
the light had descended of itself into his heart.
. . . He had taken his heart from his breast, and
given it to Him who spoke to him; and He who
spoke to him," who is the Divine, uncreated Word
of God, "filled him with deific splendor." No one
could doubt it who has had the happiness of as-
sisting at any of the catechisms of Ars; of hearing
that extraordinary language, which was like no
human language; who has seen the irresistible effect produced upon hearers of all classes by that
voice, that emotion, that intuition, that fire, and
the signal beauty of that unpolished and almost
vulgar French, which was transfigured and
penetrated by his holy energy, even to the form,
the arrangement, and the harmony of its words
and syllables. And yet the Curé of Ars did not

speak *words:* true eloquence consists in speaking things; he spoke things, and in a most wonderful manner. He poured out his whole soul into the souls of the crowds who listened to him, that he might make them believe, love, and hope like himself. That is the aim and the triumph of evangelical eloquence.

How could this man, who had nearly been refused admittance into the great seminary because of his ignorance, and who had, since his promotion to the priesthood, been solely employed in prayer and in the labors of the confessional— how could he have attained to the power of teaching like one of the Fathers of the Church? Whence did he derive his astonishing knowledge of God, of nature, and of the history of the soul? How was it that his thoughts and expressions so often coincided with those of the greatest Christian geniuses, St. Augustine, St. Bernard, St. Thomas Aquinas, St. Catherine of Siena, St. Teresa?

For example, we have often heard him say that the heart of the saints was *liquid.* We were much struck with this energetic expression, without suspecting that it was so theologically accurate; and we were surprised and touched to find, in turning over the pages of the *Summa,* that the angelical doctor assigns to love four immediate effects, of which the first is the *liquefaction* of the heart. M. Vianney had certainly never read St. Thomas, which makes this coincidence the more remarkable; and, indeed, it is inexplicable to those who are ignorant of the workings of grace, and who do not comprehend those words of the Divine Master: "Thou hast hid these things from the wise and prudent, and hast revealed them to little ones." [*Matt*. 11:25].

The Spirit of God had been pleased to engrave on the heart of this holy priest all that he was to know and to teach to others; and it was the more deeply engraved, as that heart was the more pure, the more detached, and empty of the vain science of men; like a clean and polished block of marble, ready for the tool of the sculptor.

The faith of the Curé of Ars was his whole science; his book was Our Lord Jesus Christ. He sought for wisdom nowhere but in Jesus Christ, in His death and in His Cross. To him no other wisdom was true, no other wisdom useful. He sought it not amid the dust of libraries, not in the schools of the learned, but in prayer, on his knees, at his Master's Feet, covering His Divine Feet with tears and kisses. In the presence of the Blessed Sacrament where he passed his days and nights before the crowd of pilgrims had yet deprived him of liberty day and night, he had learnt it all.

When persons have heard him discourse upon Heaven, on the Sacred Humanity of Our Lord, on His dolorous Passion, His Real Presence in the most Holy Sacrament of our altars, on the Blessed Virgin Mary, her attractions and her greatness, on the happiness of the saints, the purity of the angels, the beauty of souls, the dignity of man—on all those subjects which were familiar to him—it often happened to them to come out from the discourse quite convinced that the good father *saw* the things of which he had spoken with such fullness of heart, with such eloquent emotion, in such passionate accents, with such abundance of tears; and indeed his words were then impressed with a character of divine tenderness, of sweet gentleness, and of penetrating unction, which was beyond all comparison. There was so extraordinary a majesty, so marvelous a power, in his voice, in his gestures, in his looks, in his transfigured countenance, that it was impossible to listen to him and remain cold and unmoved.

Views and thoughts imparted by a divine light have quite a different bearing from those acquired by study. Doubt was dispelled from the most rebellious hearts, and the admirable clearness of faith took its place before so absolute a certainty, an exposition at once so luminous and so simple.

The word of the Curé of Ars was the more efficacious because he preached with his whole being. His mere presence was a manifestation of the Truth; and of him it might well be said that he would have moved and convinced men even by his silence. When there appeared in the pulpit that pale, thin, and transparent face; when you heard that shrill, piercing voice, like a cry, giving out to the crowd sublime thoughts clothed in simple and popular language, you fancied yourself in the presence of one of those great characters of the Bible, speaking to men in the language of the prophets. You were already filled with respect and confidence, and disposed to listen, not for enjoyment, but for profit.

Before he began, the venerable catechist used to cast a glance over his hearers, which prepared the way for his word. Sometimes this glance became fixed on someone; it seemed to be searching into the depths of some soul which the saint had suddenly seen through, and in which one would have thought he was looking for the text of his discourse. How many have thought he was speaking to them alone! How many have recognized themselves in the picture he drew of their weaknesses! How many have listened to the secret history of their failings, of their temptations, of their combats, of their uneasiness, and of their remorse!

To those to whom it was given to assist at these catechisms, two things were equally remarkable— the preacher and the hearer. It was not words that the preacher gave forth, it was more than words; it was a soul, a holy soul, all filled with faith and love, that poured itself out before you, of which you felt in your own soul the immediate contact and the warmth. As for the hearer, he was no longer on the earth, he was transported into those pure regions from which dogmas and mysteries descend. As the saint spoke, new and clear views opened to the mind: Heaven and earth, the present and the future life, the things of time and of eternity, appeared in a light that you had never before perceived.

When a man, coming fresh from the world,

and bringing with him worldly ideas, feelings, and impressions, sat down to listen to this doctrine, it stunned and amazed him; it set so utterly at defiance the world, and all that the world believes, loves and extols. At first he was astonished and thunderstruck; then by degrees he was touched, and surprised into weeping like the rest. No eloquence has drawn forth more tears, or penetrated deeper into the hearts of men. His words opened a way before them like flames, and the most hardened hearts melted like wax before the fire. They were burning, radiating, triumphant; they did more than charm the mind, they subdued the whole soul and brought it back to God, not by the long and difficult way of argument, but by the paths of emotion which lead shortly and directly to the desired end.

M. Vianney was listened to as a new apostle, sent by Jesus Christ to His Church, to renew in Her the holiness and fervor of His Divine Spirit, in an age whose corruption had so effaced them from the souls of most men. And it is a great marvel that, proposing, like the apostles, a doctrine incomprehensible to human reason, and very bitter to the depraved taste of the world—speaking of nothing but crosses, humiliations, poverty, and penance—his doctrine was so well received. Those who had not yet received it into their hearts were glad to feed their minds upon it. If they had not courage to make it the rule of their conduct, they could not help admiring and wishing to follow it.

It is not less remarkable that, though he spoke

only in the incorrect and common French natural to the people brought up in the country, one might say of him as of the Apostles, that he was heard by all the nations of the world, and that his voice resounded through all the earth. He was the oracle that people went to consult, that they might learn to know Jesus Christ. Not only the simple but the learned, not only the fervent but the indifferent, found in it a divine unction which penetrated them and made them long to hear it again. The more they heard, the more they wished to hear; and they always came back with love to the foot of that pulpit, as to a place where they had found beauty and truth. Nothing more clearly showed that the Curé of Ars was full of the Spirit of God, who alone is greater than our heart; we may draw from His depths without ever exhausting them, and the divine satiety which He gives only excites a greater appetite.

The holy Curé spoke without any other preparation than his continual union with God; he passed without any interval or delay from the confessional to the pulpit; and yet he showed an imperturbable confidence, which sprang from complete and absolute forgetfulness of himself. Besides, no one was tempted to criticize him. People generally criticize those who are not indifferent to their opinion of them. Those who heard the Curé of Ars had something else to do—they had to pass judgment on themselves.

M. Vianney cared nothing for what might be said or thought of him. Of whomsoever his audience might consist, though bishops and other illustrious personages often mingled with the crowd that surrounded his pulpit, he never betrayed the least emotion, nor the least embarrassment proceeding from human respect. He, who was so timid and so humble, was no longer the same person when he passed through the compact mass that filled the church at the hour of catechism; he wore an air of triumph, he carried his head high, his face was lighted up, and his eyes cast brilliant glances.

He was asked one day if he had never been afraid of his audience. "No," he answered; "on the contrary, the more people there are, the better I am pleased." Then, to impose on us, he added, "A proud man always thinks he does well." If he had had the pope, the cardinals, and kings around his pulpit, he would have said neither more nor less, for he thought only of souls, and made them think only of God. This real power of his word supplied in him the want of talent and rhetoric; it gave a singular majesty and an irresistible authority to the most simple things that issued from that venerable mouth.

The power of his word was also increased by the high opinion the pilgrims entertained of his sanctity. "The first quality of the man called to the perilous honor of instructing the people," says St. Isidore, "is to be holy and irreproachable. He whose mission it is to deter others from sin must be a stranger to sin; he whose task it is to lead others to perfection must be in everything their model of perfection." In the holy catechist of Ars, virtue was preaching truth. When he spoke of the love of God, of humility, gentleness, patience, mortification, sacrifice, poverty, or the desire of suffering, his example gave immense weight to his words; for a man who practices what he teaches is very powerful in convincing and persuading others.

He used to put his ideas into the most simple and transparent form, letting them suggest the expression that best suited them. He could bring truths of the highest order within the reach of every intellect; he clothed them in familiar language; his simplicity touched the heart, and his doctrine delighted the mind. That science which is not sought for is abundant; it flows like the fountain of living water, which the Samaritan woman knew not, and of which the Saviour taught her the virtue. Thus, his considerations on sin, on the offense it is against God, and the evil it inflicts on man, were the painful result of his thoughts. They penetrated him, they overwhelmed him; they were like a burning arrow piercing his breast; he relieved his pain by giving utterance to it.

It was a wonderful thing that this man, so ready to proclaim his own ignorance, had by nature a great attraction for the higher faculties of the mind. The greatest praise that he could give anyone was to say that he was clever. When the good qualities of any great person, whether an ecclesiastic or a layman, were enumerated before him, he seldom failed to complete the panegyric in these words: "What pleases me most is that he is learned."

M. Vianney appreciated the gift of eloquence in others; he blessed God, who for His own glory gives such privileges to man, but he disdained them for himself. He had no scruple in utterly neglecting grammar and syntax in his discourses; he seemed to do it on purpose, out of humility, for there were faults in them that he might easily have avoided. But this incorrect language penetrated the souls of his hearers, enlightened and converted them. "A polished discourse," says St. Jerome, "only gratifies the ears; one which is not so makes its way to the heart."

His manner of speaking was sudden and impetuous; he loosed his words like arrows from a bow, and his whole soul seemed to fly with them. In these effusions the pathetic, the profound, the sublime, was often side by side with the simple and vulgar. They had all the freedom and irregularity, but also all the originality and power of an improvisation. We have sometimes tried to write down what we had just heard, but it was impossible to recall the things that had most moved us and to put them into form. What is most divine in the heart of man cannot be expressed in writing. We have, however, set down a few words, in which we find more than a remembrance. We find the Curé of Ars himself, the simple expression of his heart and of his soul. These are some of his lofty and deep thoughts:

"To love God! oh how beautiful it is! We must be in Heaven to comprehend love. . . . Prayer helps us a little, because prayer is the elevation of the soul to Heaven. . . . The more we know men, the less we love them. It is the reverse with God; the more we know Him, the more we love Him. This knowledge inflames the soul with such a love, that it can no longer love or desire anything from God. . . . Man was created by love; therefore he is so disposed to love. On the other hand, he is so great that nothing on the earth can satisfy him. He can be satisfied only when he turns towards God. . . . Take a fish out of the water, and it will not live. Well, such is man without God.

"There are some who do not love the good God, who do not pray to Him, and who prosper; that is a bad sign. They have done a little good in the midst of a great deal of evil. The good God rewards them in this life.

"This earth is a bridge to cross the water; it serves only to support our steps. . . . We are in this world, but we are not of this world, since we say every day, 'Our Father, Who art in Heaven.' We must wait, then, for our reward till we are *at home*, in our Father's house. This is the reason why good Christians suffer crosses, contradictions, adversities, contempt, calumnies—so much the better! . . . But people are astonished at this. They seem to think that because we love the good God a little, we ought to have nothing to contradict us, nothing to make us suffer. . . . We say, 'There is a person who is not good, and yet everything goes well with him; but with me, it is of no use doing my best; everything goes wrong. It is because we do not understand the value and the happiness of crosses. We say sometimes that God chastises those whom He loves. That is not true. Trials are not chastisements; they are graces to those whom God loves. . . .We must not consider the labor, but the recompense. A merchant does not consider the trouble he undergoes in his commerce, but the profit he gains by it. . . .What are twenty years, thirty years, compared to eternity? What, then, have we to suffer? A few humiliations, a few annoyances, a few sharp words; *that will not kill us.*

"It is glorious to be able to please God, so little as we are! Our tongue should be employed only in praying, our heart in loving, our eyes in weeping. We are great, and we are nothing. . . .There is nothing greater than man, and nothing less. Nothing is greater, if we consider his soul; nothing is less, if we look at his body. . . .We occupy ourselves with the body, as if we had it alone to take care of; we have, on the contrary, it alone to despise. . . .We are the work of a God. . . .one always loves one's own work. . . .It is easy enough to understand that we are the work of a God; but that the crucifixion of a God should be our work! that is incomprehensible.

"Some people attribute a hard heart to the Eternal Father. Oh, how mistaken they are! The Eternal Father, to disarm His own justice, gave to

His Son an excessively tender heart; no one can give what he does not possess. Our Lord said to His Father: 'Father, do not punish them!' . . . Our Lord suffered more than was necessary to redeem us. But what would have satisfied the justice of His Father would not have satisfied His love. Without Our Lord's death, all mankind together could not expiate a single little lie.

"In the world, people hide Heaven and Hell: Heaven, because if we knew its beauty, we should wish to go there at all costs—we should, indeed, leave the world alone; Hell, because if we knew the torments that are endured there, we should do all we could to avoid going there.

"The Sign of the Cross is formidable to the devil, because by the Cross we escape from him. We should make the Sign of the Cross with great respect. We begin with the forehead: it is the head, creation—the Father; then the heart: love, life, redemption—the Son; then the shoulders: strength—the Holy Ghost. Everything reminds us of the Cross. We ourselves are made in the form of a cross. In Heaven we shall be nourished by the breath of God. . . . The good God will place us as an architect places the stones of a building—each one in the spot to which it is adapted. The soul of the saints contained the foundations of Heaven. They felt an emanation from Heaven, in which they bathed and lost themselves. . . . As the disciples on Mount Thabor saw nothing but Jesus alone, so interior souls, on the Thabor of their hearts, no longer see anything but Our Lord. They are two friends, who are never tired of each other. . . .

"There are some who lose the faith, and never see Hell till they enter it. The lost will be enveloped in the wrath of God, as the fish are in the water. It is not God who condemns us to Hell; it is we ourselves who do it by our sins. The lost do not accuse God; they accuse themselves. They say, 'I have lost God, my soul, and Heaven by my own fault.' No one was ever lost for having done too much evil; but many are in Hell for a single mortal sin of which they would not repent. If a lost soul could say once, 'O my God I love Thee!' there would be no more Hell for him...but, alas, poor soul! it has lost the power of loving which it had received, and of which it made no use. Its heart is dried up like grapes that have passed through the winepress. No more joy in that soul, no more peace, because there is no more love. . . . Hell has its origin in the goodness of God. The lost will say, 'Oh, if at least God had not loved us so much, we should suffer less! Hell would be endurable. . . . But to have been so much loved! what grief!"

Besides these deep thoughts, he had some that were forcible and startling. He called the cemetery, the home of all; Purgatory, the infirmary of the good God; the earth, a warehouse. "We are on the earth," he said, "only as in a warehouse, for a very little moment. . . . We seem not to move, and we are going toward eternity as if by steam.

"A dying man was asked what should be put on his tomb. He answered, 'You shall put, Here lies a fool, who went out of this world without knowing how he came into it.' If the poor lost souls had the time that we waste, what good use they would make of it! If they had only half-an-hour, that half-hour would depopulate Hell. In dying, we make restitution; we restore to the earth what it gave us—a little pinch of dust, the size of a nut; that is what we shall become. There is, indeed, much to be proud of in that! For our body, death is only a cleansing. In this world we must labor, we must fight. We shall have plenty of time to rest in all eternity.

"If we understood our happiness aright, we might almost say that we are happier than the saints in Heaven. They live upon their income; they can earn no more, while we can augment our treasure every moment. The Commandments of God are the guides which God gives us to show us the road to Heaven, like the names written up at the corners of the streets and on guideposts, to point out the way. The grace of God helps us to walk and supports us. He is as necessary to us as crutches are to a lame man.

"When we go to confession, we ought to understand what we are going to do. It might be said that we are going to unfasten Our Lord from the Cross. When you have made a good confession, you have chained up the devil. The sins that we conceal will all come to light.

"In order to conceal our sins effectually, we

must confess them thoroughly. Our faults are like a grain of sand beside the great mountain of the mercies of the good God."

M. Vianney made great use of comparisons and similes in his teachings; he borrowed them from nature, which was known and loved by the crowd whom he addressed, from the beauties of the country, from the emotions of rural life. The recollections of his childhood had kept all their freshness, and in his old age he could not resist the innocent pleasure of recalling for a moment the lively sympathies of his youth. This return of the thoughts to the brightest days of life is like an anticipation of the Resurrection. After the manner of Our Lord, he used the most well-known events, the most common facts, the incidents that came before him as figures of the spiritual life, and made them the theme of his instructions. The Gospel is full of symbols and figures, fitted to lead the soul to the comprehension of eternal truths by a comparison with what is more evident to the senses. In like manner, allusions, metaphors, parables and figures colored all the discourses of the Curé of Ars. His mind had acquired the habit of raising itself, by means of visible things, to God and to the invisible. There was not one of his catechisms in which he did not often speak of rivulets, forests, trees, birds, flowers, dew, lilies, balm, perfume and honey. All contemplatives love this language, and the innocence of their thoughts attaches itself by predilection to all the beautiful and pure things with which the Author of creation has embellished His work. A good man, Our Lord says, brings forth good things out of the good treasures of his heart. The sweet writings of St. Francis of Sales are a model of this style, dear to all mystics; and we are not surprised to find these graces of language and this exquisite taste in the Bishop of Geneva. But where had this poor country curé learnt his flowers of eloquence? Who had taught him to use them with such delicate tact and ingenuity? Let us listen:

"Like a beautiful white dove rising from the midst of the waters, and coming to shake her wings over the earth, the Holy Spirit issues from the infinite ocean of the Divine perfections, and hovers over pure souls, to pour into them the balm of love. The Holy Spirit reposes in a pure soul as on a bed of roses. There comes forth from a soul in which the Holy Spirit resides a sweet odor, like that of the vine when it is in flower.

"He who has preserved his baptismal innocence is like a child who has never disobeyed his father. . . . One who has kept his innocence feels himself lifted up on high by love, as a bird is carried up by its wings. Those who have pure souls are like eagles and swallows, which fly in the air. . . . A Christian who is pure is upon earth like a bird that is kept fastened down by a string. Poor little bird! it only waits for the moment when the string is cut to fly away.

"Good Christians are like those birds that have large wings and small feet, and which never light upon the ground, because they could not rise again and would be caught. They make their nests, too, upon the points of rocks, on the roofs of houses, in high places. So the Christian ought to be always on the heights. As soon as we lower our thoughts towards the earth, we are taken captive.

"A pure soul is like a fine pearl. As long as it is hidden in the shell, at the bottom of the sea, no one thinks of admiring it. But if you bring it into the sunshine, this pearl will shine and attract all eyes. Thus, the pure soul, which is hidden from the eyes of the world, will one day shine before the angels in the sunshine of eternity. The pure soul is a beautiful rose, and the Three Divine Persons descend from Heaven to inhale its fragrance.

"The mercy of God is like an overflowing torrent—it carries away hearts with it as it passes. The good God will pardon a repentant sinner more quickly than a mother would snatch her child out of the fire. The elect are like the ears of corn that are left by the reapers, and like the bunches of grapes after the vintage. Imagine a poor mother obliged to let fall the blade of the guillotine upon the head of her child: such is the good God when He condemns a sinner.

"What happiness will it be for the just, at the end of the world, when the soul, perfumed with the odors of Heaven, shall be reunited to its body, and enjoy God for all eternity! Then our bodies will come out of the ground like linen that has been bleached. . . .The bodies of the just will shine in Heaven like fine diamonds, like globes of love!

What a cry of joy when the soul shall come to unite itself to its glorified body—to that body which will never more be to it an instrument of sin, nor a cause of suffering! It will revel in the sweetness of love, as the bee revels in flowers. ...Thus the soul will be embalmed for eternity!"

We see that the Curé of Ars was a poet, in the highest sense of the word; his heart was endowed with exquisite sensibility, and he gave expression to it in the simplest and truest manner.

"One day in spring," he said, "I was going to see a sick person; the bushes were full of little birds that were singing with all their might. I took pleasure in listening to them, and I said to myself, 'Poor little birds, you know not what you are doing! What a pity that is! You are singing the praises of God." Does not this recall St. Francis of Assisi?

"Our holy Curé," writes one of his most intelligent hearers, "is always equally admirable in his life, his works, and his words. This may perhaps surprise you, but it is perfectly true. There is something astonishing in the satisfaction, or rather the enthusiasm, with which the crowd of all classes presses in to hear his so-called catechisms. I have heard distinguished ecclesiastics, men of the world, learned men, and artists, declare that nothing had ever touched them so much as that expansion of a heart that is contemplating, loving, and adoring. A collection might almost be made of the *Fioretti* of the Curé of Ars. Nothing could be more graceful and brilliant than the picture he drew, a few days ago, of spring."

A few lines further on, he added, "Yesterday, our old St. Francis of Assisi was more poetical than ever, in the midst of his tears and of his bursts of love. Speaking of the soul of man, which ought to aspire to God alone, he cried out, 'Does the fish seek the trees and the fields? No; it darts through the water. Does the bird remain on the earth? No; it flies in the air. . . . And man, who is created to love God, to possess God, to contain God, what will he do with all the powers that have been given to him for that end?'"

He liked to relate the simple and poetic legend of St. Maur, who, when he was one day carrying St. Benedict his dinner, found a large serpent. He took it up, put it in the fold of his habit, and showed it to St. Benedict, saying, "See, Father, what I have found." When the holy patriarch and all the religious were assembled, the serpent began to hiss, and tried to bite them. Then St. Benedict said, "My child, go back, and put it where you found it." And when St. Maur was gone, he added, "My brethren, do you know why that animal is so gentle with that child? It is because he has kept his baptismal innocence."

He also repeated with great pleasure the anecdote of St. Francis of Assisi preaching to the fishes. "One day," he said, "St. Francis of Assisi was preaching in a province where there were a great many heretics. These miscreants stopped their ears to avoid hearing him. The saint then led the people to the seashore, and called the fishes to come and listen to the Word of God, since men rejected it. The fishes came to the edge of the water, the large ones behind the little ones. St. Francis asked them this question, 'Are you grateful to the good God for saving you from the deluge?' The fishes bowed their heads. Then St. Francis said to the people, 'See, these fishes are grateful for the benefits of God, and you are so ungrateful as to despise them!'"

M. Vianney mingled with his discourses some happy reminiscenses of his shepherd's life: "We ought to do like shepherds who are in the fields in winter—life is indeed a long winter. They kindle a fire, but from time to time they run about in all directions to look for wood to keep it up. If we, like the shepherds, were always to keep up the fire of the love of God in our hearts by prayers and good works, it would never go out. If you have not the love of God, you are very poor. You are like a tree without flowers or fruit. It is always springtime in a soul united to God." When he spoke of prayer, the most pleasing and ingenious comparisons fell abundantly from his lips: "Prayer is a fragrant dew; but we must pray with a pure heart to feel this dew. There flows from prayer a delicious sweetness like the juice of very ripe grapes. Prayer disengages our soul from matter; it raises it on high, like the fire that inflates a balloon.

"The more we pray, the more we wish to pray.

Like a fish which at first swims on the surface of the water, and afterwards plunges down, and is always going deeper, the soul plunges, dives, and loses itself in the sweetness of conversing with God. Time never seems long in prayer. I know not whether we can even wish for Heaven? Oh, yes! . . . The fish swimming in a little rivulet is well off, because it is in its element; but it is still better in the sea. When we pray, we should open our heart to God, like a fish when it sees the wave coming. The good God has no need of us. He commands us to pray only because He wills our happiness, and our happiness can be found only in prayer. When He sees us coming, He bends His heart down very low towards His little creature, as a father bends down to listen to his little child when it speaks to him.

"In the morning, we must do like the little child in its cradle. The moment it opens its eyes, it looks round the house for its mother. When it sees her, it begins to smile; if it does not see her, it cries." Speaking of the priest, he made use of this touching simile:

"The priest is like a mother to you, like a nurse to a child of a few months old. She feeds it—it has only to open its mouth. The mother says to her child, 'Here my little one, eat.' The priest says to you, 'Take and eat; this is the Body of Jesus Christ. May it keep you, and lead you to life eternal.' Oh, beautiful words! 'A child struggles against anyone who keeps it back; it opens its little mouth, and stretches out its little arms to embrace her. Your soul, in the presence of the priest, naturally springs towards him; it runs to meet him; but it is held back by the bonds of the flesh, in men who give everything to the senses, who live only for their body.

"Our soul is swathed in our body, like a baby in its swaddling-clothes; we can see nothing but its face." Everyone will be struck with the truth and aptitude of this last simile. Besides these touching comparisons, some of M. Vianney's were original and energetic. To exalt the benefits of the Sacrament of Penance, he made use of metaphors and parables: "A furious wolf once came into our country, devouring everything. Finding on his way a child of two years old, he seized it in his mouth, and carried it off; but some men, who were pruning a vineyard, ran to attack him, and snatched his prey from him. It is thus that the Sacrament of Penance snatches us from the claws of the devil."

When he had to draw a parallel between Christians and worldly people, he said, "I think none so much to be pitied as those poor worldly people. They wear a cloak lined with thorns—they cannot move without pricking themselves; while good Christians have a cloak lined with soft fur. The good Christian sets no value on the goods of this world. He escapes from them like a rat out of the water.

"Unhappily, our hearts are not sufficiently pure and free from all earthly affections. If you take a very clean and very dry sponge, and soak it in water, it will be filled to overflowing; but if it is not dry and clean, it will take up nothing. In like manner, when the heart is not free and disengaged from the things of the earth, it is in vain that we steep it in prayer; it will absorb nothing.

"The heart of the wicked swarms with sins like an anthill with ants. It is like a piece of bad meat full of worms. When we abandon ourselves to our passions, we interweave thorns around our heart. We are like moles a week old; no sooner do we see the light, than we bury ourselves in the ground. The devil amuses us till the last moment, as a poor man is kept amused while the soldiers are coming to take him. When they come, he cries and struggles in vain, for they will not release him.

"When men die, they are often like a very rusty bar of iron, that must be put into the fire. Poor sinners are stupefied like snakes in winter. The slanderer is like the snail, which crawling over flowers, leaves its slime upon them and defiles them. What would you say of a man who should plough his neighbor's field, and leave his own uncultivated? Well, that is what you do. You are always at work on the consciences of others, and you leave your own untilled. Oh, when death comes, how we shall regret having thought so much of others, and so little of ourselves; for we shall have to give an account of ourselves, and not of others! Let us think of ourselves, of our own conscience, which we ought always to examine, as we examine our hands to see if they are clean.

"We always have two secretaries: the devil, who writes down our bad actions, to accuse us of them; and our good angel, who writes down our good ones, to justify us at the Day of Judgment. When all our actions shall be brought before us, how few will be pleasing to God, even among the best of them! So many imperfections, so many thoughts of self-love, human satisfactions, sensual pleasures, self-complacency, will be found mingled with them all! They appear good, but it is only appearance, like those fruits which seem yellow and ripe because they have been pierced by insects."

We see by these fragments that M. Vianney was one of those contemplatives who do not disdain to soften the austerity of their ideas by simple graces of expression, whether out of compassionate kindness to their disciples, or from the natural attraction felt by those who are good for what is beautiful. He found in beautiful creatures Him who is supremely beautiful; he disdained not the least of them. At peace with all things, and having returned in a manner to the primitive innocence and condition of Eden, when Adam beheld creatures in the divine light, and loved them with fraternal charity, his heart overflowed with love, not only for men, but also for all beings visible and invisible. His words breathed an affectionate sympathy for the whole of creation, which no doubt appeared to him in its original dignity and purity. He looked upon it as a sister, who expressed the same thoughts and the same love as himself in another manner. This is shown in his apostrophe to the little birds. Where other eyes perceived nothing but perishable beauties, he discovered, as with a sort of second sight, the holy harmony and the eternal relations which connect the physical with the moral order—the mysteries of nature with those of faith. He did the same in the region of history. Ages, events, and men were to him only symbols and allegories, prophecies and their accomplishment.

Nothing could be more beautiful, touching, and pathetic, than the application that he made of the legend of St. Alexis to the Real Presence of Our Lord. At the moment when the mother of St. Alexis recognizes her son in the lifeless body of the beggar, who has lived thirty years under the staircase of her palace, she cries out, "O my son, why have I known thee so late?"...The soul, on quitting this life, will see Him whom it possessed in the Holy Eucharist; and at the sight of the consolations, of the beauty, of the riches that it failed to recognize, it also will cry out, "O Jesus! O my God! why have I known Thee so late."

The Curé of Ars sometimes made edifying reflections on recent events and circumstances which had made an impression upon himself; and, though he did it with reserve, we have in this way gained some valuable information, which would otherwise have been lost. "Because Our Lord does not show Himself in the most Holy Sacrament in all His majesty you behave without respect in His Presence; but, nevertheless, He Himself is there. He is in the midst of you. . . . So, when that good bishop was here the other day, everybody was pushing against him . . . Ah, if they had known he was a bishop! . . .

"We give our youth to the devil, and the remains of our life to the Good God, who is so good that He deigns to be content with even that . . . but, happily, everyone does not do so. A great lady has been here, of one of the first families in France; she went away this morning. She is scarcely three-and-twenty, and she is rich—very rich indeed. . . . She has offered herself in sacrifice to the good God for the expiation of sins, and for the conversion of sinners. She wears a girdle all armed with iron points; she mortifies herself in a thousand ways; and her parents know nothing of it. She is white as a sheet of paper. Hers is a beautiful soul, very pleasing to the good God, such as are still to be found now and then in the world, and they prevent the world from coming to an end.

"One day, two Protestant ministers came here, who did not believe in the Real Presence of Our Lord. I said to them, 'Do you think that a piece of bread could detach itself, and go, of its own accord, to place itself on the tongue of a person who came near to receive it?' 'No.' 'Then it is not bread.' There was a man who had doubts about the Real Presence, and he said, 'What do we know about it? It is not certain. What is consecration? What happens on the altar at that moment?' But he wished to believe, and he prayed the Blessed Virgin to obtain faith for him. Listen attentively to this. I do not say that this happened somewhere, but I say that it happened to myself. *At the moment when this man came up to receive Holy Communion, the Sacred Host detached Itself from my fingers while I was still a good way off, and went off Itself and placed Itself upon the tongue of that man."*

We will not undertake to give a consecutive view of the teaching of the Curé of Ars. There was indeed a sort of connection between the parts of it, but it would be impossible to describe the sudden inspirations that burst forth and ran through it like rays of light. His Catechisms in general defied analysis; and we should be afraid of disfiguring them by reducing them to the formality of a theological system. We shall therefore confine ourselves to offering to our readers an abridgment of some of the most remarkable discourses.

The
Little Catechism
of the
Curé of Ars

— Part I —

INSTRUCTIONS ON THE CATECHISM

*The Spirit of the Curé of Ars
St. John Mary Vianney*

CHAPTER 1

Catechism on Salvation

THERE ARE many Christians who do not even know why they are in the world. "Oh my God, why hast Thou sent me into the world?" "To save your soul." "And why dost Thou wish me to be saved?" "Because I love you." The good God has created us and sent us into the world because He loves us; He wishes to save us because He loves us. . . .To be saved, we must know, love and serve God. Oh, what a beautiful life! How good, how great a thing it is to know, to love and serve God! We have nothing else to do in this world. All that we do besides is lost time. We must act only for God, and put our works into His hands. . . .We should say, on awaking, "I desire to do everything today for Thee, O my God! I will submit to all that Thou shalt send me, as coming from Thee. I offer myself as a sacrifice to Thee. But, O God, I can do nothing without Thee. Do Thou help me!"

Oh, how bitterly shall we regret at the hour of death the time we have given to pleasures, to useless conversations, to repose, instead of having employed it in mortification, in prayer, in good works, in thinking of our poor misery, in weeping over our poor sins; then we shall see that we have done nothing for Heaven. Oh, my children, how sad it is! Three-quarters of those who are Christians labor for nothing but to satisfy this body, which will soon be buried and corrupted, while they do not give a thought to their poor soul, which must be happy or miserable for all eternity. They have neither sense nor reason: it makes one tremble.

Look at that man, who is so active and restless, who makes a noise in the world, who wants to govern everybody, who thinks himself of consequence, who seems as if he would like to say to the sun, "Go away, and let me enlighten the world instead of you." Someday this proud man will be reduced at the utmost to a little handful of dust, which will be swept away from river to river, from Saone to Saone, and at last into the sea.

See my children, I often think that we are like those little heaps of sand that the wind raises on the road, which whirl round for a moment, and are scattered directly. . . .We have brothers and sisters who are dead. Well, they are reduced to that little handful of dust of which I was speaking. Worldly people say, it is too difficult to save one's soul. Yet nothing is easier. To observe the Commandments of God and the Church, and to avoid the seven capital sins; or if you like to put it so, to do good and avoid evil: that is all. Good Christians, who labor to save their souls and to work out their salvation, are always happy and contented; they enjoy beforehand the happiness of Heaven: they will be happy for all eternity.

While bad Christians, who lose their souls, are always to be pitied; they murmur, they are sad, they are as miserable as stones; and they will be so for all eternity. See what a difference!

This is a good rule of conduct, to do nothing but what we can offer to the good God. Now, we cannot offer to Him slanders, calumnies, injustice, anger, blasphemy, impurity, theaters, dancing; yet that is all that people do in the world. Speaking of dances, St. Francis of Sales used to say that "they were like mushrooms, the best were good for nothing." Mothers are apt to say indeed, "Oh, I watch over my daughters." They watch over their attire, but they cannot watch over their hearts. Those who have dances in their houses load themselves with a terrible responsibility before God; they are answerable for all the evil that is done—for the bad thoughts, the slanders, the jealousies, the hatred, the revenge. . . . Ah, if they well understood this responsibility they would never have any dances. Just like those who make bad pictures and statues, or write bad books, they will have to answer for all the harm that these things will do during all the time they last. . . . Oh that makes one tremble!

See, my children, we must reflect that we have a soul to save, and an eternity that awaits us. The world, its riches, pleasures, and honors will pass away. Let us take care, then. The saints did not all begin well; but they all ended well. We have begun badly; let us end well, and we shall go one day and meet them in Heaven.

CHAPTER 2

Catechism on The Love of God

OUR BODY is a vessel of corruption; it is meant for death and for the worms, nothing more! And yet we devote ourselves to satisfying it, rather than to enriching our soul, which is so great that we can conceive nothing greater— no, nothing, nothing! For we see that God, urged by the ardor of His charity, would not create us like the animals; He has created us in His own image and likeness, do you see? Oh, how great is man?

Man, being created by love, cannot live without love: either he loves God, or he loves himself and he loves the world. See, my children, it is faith that we want. . . .When we have not faith, we are blind. He who does not see, does not know; he who does not know does not love; he who does not love God loves himself, and at the same time loves his pleasures. He fixes his heart on things which pass away like smoke. He cannot know the truth, nor any good thing; he can know nothing but falsehood, because he has no light; he is in a mist. If he had light, he would see plainly that all that he loves can give him nothing but eternal death; it is a foretaste of Hell.

Do you see, my children, except God, nothing is solid—nothing, nothing! If it is life, it passes away; if it is a fortune, it crumbles away; if it is health, it is destroyed; if it is reputation, it is attacked. We are scattered like the wind. . . . Everything is passing away full speed, everything is going to ruin. O God! O God! how much those are to be pitied, then, who set their hearts on all these things! They set their hearts on them because they love themselves too much; but they do not love themselves with a reasonable love— they love themselves with a love that seeks themselves and the world, that seeks creatures more than God. That is the reason why they are never satisfied, never quiet; they are always uneasy, always tormented, always upset. See, my children, the good Christian runs his course in this world mounted on a fine triumphal chariot; this chariot is borne by angels, and conducted by Our Lord Himself, while the poor sinner is harnessed to the chariot of this life, and the devil who drives it forces him to go on with great strokes of the whip.

My children, the three acts of faith, hope and charity contain all the happiness of man upon the earth. By faith, we believe what God has promised us: we believe that we shall one day see Him, that we shall possess Him, that we shall be eternally happy with Him in Heaven. By hope, we expect the fulfillment of these promises: we hope that we shall be rewarded for all our good actions, for all our good thoughts, for all our good desires; for God takes into account even our good desires. What more do we want to make us happy?

In Heaven, faith and hope will exist no more, for the mist which obscures our reason will be dispelled; our mind will be able to understand the things that are hidden from it here below. We shall no longer hope for anything, because we shall have everything. We do not hope to acquire a treasure which we already possess. . . . But love; oh, we shall be inebriated with it! we shall be drowned, lost in that ocean of divine love, annihilated in that immense charity of the Heart of Jesus! so that charity is a foretaste of Heaven. Oh, how happy should we be if we knew how to understand it, to feel it, to taste it! What makes us unhappy is that we do not love God.

When we say, "My God, I believe, I believe firmly," that is, without the least doubt, without the least hesitation. . . Oh, if we were penetrated with these words: "I firmly believe that Thou art present everywhere, that Thou seest me, that I am under Thine eyes, that one day I myself shall see Thee clearly, that I shall enjoy all the good things Thou hast promised me! O my God, I hope that Thou wilt reward me for all that I have done to please Thee! O my God, I love Thee; my heart is made to love Thee!" Oh, this act of faith, which is also an act of love, would suffice for everything! If we understood our own happiness in being able to love God, we should remain motionless in ecstasy. . . .

If a prince, an emperor, were to cause one of his subjects to appear before him, and should say to him, "I wish to make you happy; stay with me, enjoy all my possessions, but be careful not to give me any just cause of displeasure," with what care, with what ardor, would not that subject endeavor to satisfy his prince! Well, God makes the same proposals to us...and we do not care for His friendship, we make no account of His promises. ...What a pity!

CHAPTER 3

Catechism on The Holy Spirit

O MY CHILDREN, how beautiful it is! The Father is our Creator, the Son is our Redeemer, and the Holy Ghost is our Guide. ....Man by himself is nothing, but with the Holy Spirit he is very great. Man is all earthly and all animal; nothing but the Holy Spirit can elevate his mind, and raise it on high. Why were the saints so detached from the earth? Because they let themselves be led by the Holy Spirit. Those who are led by the Holy Spirit have true ideas; that is the reason why so many ignorant people are wiser than the learned. When we are led by a God of strength and light, we cannot go astray.

The Holy Spirit is light and strength. He teaches us to distinguish between truth and falsehood, and between good and evil. Like glasses that magnify objects, the Holy Spirit shows us good and evil on a large scale. With the Holy Spirit we see everything in its true proportions; we see the greatness of the least actions done for God, and the greatness of the least faults. As a watchmaker with his glasses distinguishes the most minute wheels of a watch, so we, with the light of the

Holy Ghost, distinguish all the details of our poor life. Then the smallest imperfections appear very great, the least sins inspire us with horror. That is the reason why the most Holy Virgin never sinned. The Holy Ghost made her understand the hideousness of sin; she shuddered with terror at the least fault.

Those who have the Holy Spirit cannot endure themselves, so well do they know their poor misery. The proud are those who have not the Holy Spirit.

Worldly people have not the Holy Spirit, or if they have, it is only for a moment. He does not remain with them; the noise of the world drives Him away. A Christian who is led by the Holy Spirit has no difficulty in leaving the goods of this world, to run after those of Heaven; he knows the difference between them. The eyes of the world see no further than this life, as mine see no further than this wall when the church door is shut. The eyes of the Christian see deep into eternity. To the man who gives himself up to the guidance of the Holy Ghost, there seems to be no world; to the world there seems to be no God. . . .We must therefore find out by whom we are led. If it is not by the Holy Ghost, we labor in vain; there is no substance nor savor in anything we do. If it is by the Holy Ghost, we taste a delicious sweetness. . . it is enough to make us die of pleasure!

Those who are led by the Holy Spirit experience all sorts of happiness in themselves, while bad

Christians roll themselves on thorns and flints. A soul in which the Holy Spirit dwells is never weary in the presence of God; his heart gives forth a breath of love. Without the Holy Ghost we are like the stones on the road. . . .Take in one hand a sponge full of water, and in the other a little pebble; press them equally. Nothing will come out of the pebble, but out of the sponge will come abundance of water. The sponge is the soul filled with the Holy Spirit, and the stone is the cold and hard heart which is not inhabited by the Holy Spirit.

A soul that possesses the Holy Spirit tastes such sweetness in prayer, that it finds the time always too short; it never loses the holy presence of God. Such a heart, before our good Saviour in the Holy Sacrament of the Altar, is a bunch of grapes under the wine press. The Holy Spirit forms thoughts and suggests words in the hearts of the just. . . .Those who have the Holy Spirit produce nothing bad; all the fruits of the Holy Spirit are good. Without the Holy Spirit all is cold; therefore, when we feel we are losing our fervor, we must instantly make a novena to the Holy Spirit to ask for faith and love. . . .See, when we have made a retreat or a jubilee, we are full of good desires: these good desires are the breath of the Holy Ghost, which has passed over our souls, and has renewed everything, like the warm wind which melts the ice and brings back the spring. . . .You who are not great saints, you still have many moments when you taste the sweetness of prayer and of the presence of God: these are visits of the Holy Spirit. When we have the Holy Spirit, the heart expands—bathes itself in divine love. A fish never complains of having too much water, neither does a good Christian ever complain of being too long with the good God. There are some people who find religion wearisome, and it is because they have not the Holy Spirit.

If the damned were asked: Why are you in Hell? they would answer: For having resisted the Holy Spirit. And if the saints were asked, Why are you in Heaven? they would answer: For having listened to the Holy Spirit. When good thoughts come into our minds, it is the Holy Spirit who is visiting us. The Holy Spirit is a power. The Holy Spirit supported St. Simeon on his column; He sustained the martyrs. Without the Holy Spirit, the martyrs would have fallen like the leaves from the trees. When the fires were lighted under them, the Holy Spirit extinguished the heat of the fire by the heat of divine love. The good God, in sending us the Holy Spirit, has treated us like a great king who should send his minister to guide one of his subjects, saying, "You will accompany this man everywhere, and you will bring him back to me safe and sound." How beautiful it is, my children, to be accompanied by the Holy Spirit! He is indeed a good Guide; and to think that there are some who will not follow Him. The Holy Spirit is like a man with a carriage and horse, who should want to take us to Paris. We should only have to say "yes," and to get into it. It is indeed an easy matter to say "yes"! . . .Well, the Holy Spirit wants to take us to Heaven; we have only to say "yes," and to let Him take us there.

The Holy Spirit is like a gardener cultivating our souls. . . .The Holy Spirit is our servant. . . .There is a gun; well you load it, but someone must fire it and make it go off. . . .In the same way, we have in ourselves the power of doing good. . .when the Holy Spirit gives the impulse, good works are produced. The Holy Spirit reposes in just souls like the dove in her nest. He brings out good desires in a pure soul, as the dove hatches her young ones. The Holy Spirit leads us as a mother leads by the hand her child of two years old, as a person who can see leads one who is blind.

The Sacraments which Our Lord instituted would not have saved us without the Holy Spirit. Even the death of Our Lord would have been useless to us without Him. Therefore Our Lord said to His Apostles, "It is good for you that I should go away; for if I did not go, the Consoler would not come." The descent of the Holy Ghost was required, to render fruitful that harvest of graces. It is like a grain of wheat—you cast it into the ground; yes, but it must have sun and rain to make it grow and come into ear. We should say every morning, "O God, send me Thy Spirit to teach me what I am and what Thou art."

CHAPTER 4

Catechism on the Blessed Virgin

THE FATHER takes pleasure in looking upon the heart of the most Holy Virgin Mary, as the masterpiece of His hands; for we always like our own work, especially when it is well done. The Son takes pleasure in it as the heart of His Mother, the source from which He drew the Blood that has ransomed us; the Holy Ghost as His temple. The Prophets published the glory of Mary before her birth; they compared her to the sun. Indeed, the apparition of the Holy Virgin may well be compared to a beautiful gleam of sun on a foggy day.

Before her coming, the anger of God was hanging over our heads like a sword ready to strike us. As soon as the Holy Virgin appeared upon the earth, His anger was appeased. . . . She did not know that she was to be the Mother of God, and when she was a little child she used to say, "When shall I then see that beautiful creature who is to be the Mother of God?" The Holy Virgin has brought us forth twice, in the Incarnation and at the foot of the Cross; she is then doubly our Mother. The Holy Virgin is often compared to a mother, but she is much better still than the best of mothers; for the best of mothers sometimes punishes her child when it displeases her, and even beats it: she thinks she is doing right. But the Holy Virgin does not so; she is so good that she treats us with love, and never punishes us.

The heart of this good Mother is all love and mercy; she desires only to see us happy. We have only to turn to her to be heard. The Son has His justice, the Mother has nothing but her love. God has loved us so much as to die for us; but in the heart of Our Lord there is justice, which is an attribute of God; in that of the most Holy Virgin there is nothing but mercy. Her Son being ready to punish a sinner, Mary interposes, checks the sword, implores pardon for the poor criminal. "Mother," Our Lord says to her, "I can refuse you nothing. If Hell could repent, you would obtain its pardon."

The most Holy Virgin places herself between her Son and us. The greater sinners we are, the more tenderness and compassion does she feel for us. The child that has cost its mother most tears is the dearest to her heart. Does not a mother always run to the help of the weakest and the most exposed to danger? Is not a physician in the hospital most attentive to those who are most seriously ill? The Heart of Mary is so tender towards us, that those of all the mothers in the world put together are like a piece of ice in comparison to hers. See how good the Holy Virgin is! Her great servant St. Bernard used often to say to her, "I salute thee, Mary." One day this good Mother answered him, "I salute thee, my son Bernard."

The *Ave Maria* is a prayer that is never wearisome. The devotion to the Holy Virgin is delicious, sweet, nourishing. When we talk on earthly subjects or politics, we grow weary; but when we talk of the Holy Virgin, it is always new. All the saints have a great devotion to Our Lady; no grace comes from Heaven without passing through her hands. We cannot go into a house without speaking to the porter; well, the Holy Virgin is the portress of Heaven.

When we have to offer anything to a great personage, we get it presented by the person he likes best, in order that the homage may be agreeable to him. So our prayers have quite a different sort of merit when they are presented by the Blessed Virgin, because she is the only creature who has never offended God. The Blessed Virgin alone has fulfilled the first Commandment—to adore God only, and love Him perfectly. She fulfilled it completely.

All that the Son asks of the Father is granted Him. All that the Mother asks of the Son is in like manner granted to her. When we have handled something fragrant, our hands perfume whatever they touch: let our prayers pass through the hands of the Holy Virgin; she will perfume them. I think that at the end of the world the Blessed Virgin will be very tranquil; but while the world lasts, we drag her in all directions. . . . The Holy Virgin is like a mother who has a great many children—she is continually occupied in going from one to the other.

CHAPTER 5

Catechism on The Word of God

MY CHILDREN, the Word of God is of no little importance! These were Our Lord's first words to His Apostles: "Go and teach". . . to show us that instruction is before everything.

My children, what has taught us our religion? The instructions we have heard. What gives us a horror of sin? What makes us alive to the beauty of virtue, inspires us with the desire of Heaven? Instructions. What teaches fathers and mothers the duties they have to fulfill towards their children and children the duties they have to fulfill towards their parents? Instructions.

My children, why are people so blind and so ignorant? Because they make so little account of the Word of God. There are some who do not even say a *Pater* and an *Ave* to beg of the good God the grace to listen to it attentively, and to profit well by it. I believe, my children, that a person who does not hear the Word of God as he ought, will not be saved; he will not know what to do to be saved. But with a well-instructed person there is always some resource. He may wander in all sorts of evil ways; there is still hope that he will return sooner or later to the good

18

God, even if it were only at the hour of death. Instead of which a person who has never been instructed is like a sick person—like one in his agony who is no longer conscious: he knows neither the greatness of sin nor the value of virtue; he drags himself from sin to sin, like a rag that is dragged in the mud.

See, my children, the esteem in which Our Lord holds the Word of God; to the woman who cries, "Blessed is the womb that bore Thee, and the paps that gave Thee suck!" He answers, "Yea, rather blessed are they who hear the Word of God and keep it!" Our Lord, who is Truth itself, puts no less value on His Word than on His Body. I do not know whether it is worse to have distractions during Mass than during the instructions; I see no difference. During Mass we lose the merits of the Death and Passion of Our Lord, and during the instructions we lose His Word, which is Himself. St. Augustine says that it is as bad as to take the chalice after the Consecration and to trample it underfoot.

My children, you make a scruple of missing holy Mass, because you commit a great sin in missing it by your own fault; but you have no scruple in missing an instruction. You never consider that in this way you may greatly offend God. At the Day of Judgment, when you will all be there around me, and the good God will say to you, "Give Me an account of the instructions and the catechisms which you have heard and which you might have heard," you will think very differently.

My children, you go out during the instructions, you amuse yourselves with laughing, you do not listen, you think yourselves too clever to come to the catechism . . . do you think, my children, that things will be allowed to go on so? Oh no, certainly not! God will arrange matters very differently. How sad it is! We see fathers and mothers stay outside during the instruction; yet they are under obligation to instruct their children; but how can they teach them? They are not instructed themselves. . . . All this leads straight to Hell. . . . It is a pity!

My children, I have remarked that there is no moment when people are more inclined to sleep than during the instructions. . . . You will say, I am so very sleepy. . . . If I were to take up a fiddle, nobody would think of sleeping; everybody would be roused, everybody would be on the alert. My children, you listen when you like the preacher; but if the preacher does not suit you, you turn him into ridicule. . . . We must not think so much about the man. It is not the body that we must attend to. Whatever the priest may be, he is still the instrument that the good God makes use of to distribute His holy Word. You pour liquor through a funnel; whether it be made of gold or of copper, if the liquor is good it will still be good.

There are some who go about repeating everywhere, "Priests say just what they please." No, my children, priests do not say what they please; they say what is in the Gospel. The priests who came before us said what we say; those who shall come after us will say the same thing. If we were to say things that are not true, the Bishop would very soon forbid us to preach. We say only what Our Lord has taught.

My children, I will give you an example of what it is not to believe what priests tell you. There were two soldiers passing through a place where a mission was being given; one of the soldiers proposed to his comrade to go and hear the sermon, and they went. The missionary preached upon Hell. "Do you believe all that this priest says?" asked the least wicked of the two. "Oh, no!" replied the other, "I believe it is all nonsense, invented to frighten people." "Well, for my part, I believe it; and to prove to you that I believe it, I shall give up being a soldier, and go into a convent." "Go where you please; I shall continue my journey." But while he was on his journey, he fell ill and died. The other, who was in the convent, heard of his death, and began to pray that God would show him in what state his companion had died. One day, as he was praying, his companion appeared to him; he recognized him, and asked him, "Where are you?" "In Hell; I am lost!" "O wretched man! do you now believe what the missionary said?" "Yes, I believe it. Missionaries are wrong only in one respect; they do not tell you a hundredth part of what is suffered here."

My children, I often think that most of the Christians who are lost for want of instruction—they do not know their religion well. For example, here is a person who has to go and do his day's work. This person has a desire to do great penances, to pass half the night in prayer; if he is well instructed, he will say, "No, I must not do that, because then I could not fulfill my duty tomorrow; I should be sleepy, and the least thing would put me out of patience; I should be weary all the day, and I should not do half as much work as if I had rested at night; that must not be done."

Again, my children, a servant may have a desire to fast, but he is obliged to pass the whole day in digging and ploughing, or whatever you please. Well, if this servant is well instructed, he will think, "But if I do this, I shall not be able to satisfy my master." Well, what will he do? He will eat his breakfast, and mortify himself in some other way. That is what we must do—we must always act in the way that will give most glory to the good God.

A person knows that another is in distress, and takes from his parents what will relieve that distress. He would certainly do much better to ask than to take it. If his parents refuse to give it, he will pray to God to inspire a rich person to give the alms instead of him. A well-instructed person always has two guides leading the way before him—good counsel and obedience.

CHAPTER 6

Catechism on the Prerogatives of the Pure Soul

NOTHING IS so beautiful as a pure soul. If we understood this, we could not lose our purity. The pure soul is disengaged from matter, from earthly things, and from itself. . . .That is why the saints ill-treated their body, that is why they did not grant it what it required, not even to rise five minutes later, to warm themselves, to eat anything that gave them pleasure. . . .For what the body loses the soul gains, and what the body gains the soul loses.

Purity comes from Heaven; we must ask for it from God. If we ask for it, we shall obtain it. We must take great care not to lose it. We must shut our heart against pride, against sensuality, and all the other passions, as one shuts the doors and windows that nobody may be able to get in. What joy is it to the guardian angel to conduct a pure soul! My children, when a soul is pure, all Heaven looks upon it with love! Pure souls will form the circle round Our Lord. The more pure we have been on earth, the nearer we shall be to Him in Heaven. When the heart is pure, it cannot help loving, because it has found the source of love, which is God. "Happy," says Our Lord, "are the pure in heart, because they shall see God!"

My children, we cannot comprehend the power that a pure soul has over the good God. It is not he who does the will of God, it is God who does his will. Look at Moses, that very pure soul. When God would punish the Jewish people, He said to him: Do not pray for them, because My anger must fall upon this people. Nevertheless, Moses prayed, and God spared His people; He let Himself be entreated; He could not resist the prayer of that pure soul. O my children, a soul that has never been stained by that accursed sin obtains from God whatever it wishes!

Three things are wanted to preserve purity— the presence of God, prayer, and the Sacraments. Another means is the reading of holy books, which nourishes the soul. How beautiful is a pure soul! Our Lord showed one to St. Catherine; she thought it so beautiful that she said, "O Lord, if I did not know that there is only one God, I should think it was one." The image of God is reflected in a pure soul, like the sun in the water. A pure soul is the admiration of the Three Persons of the Holy Trinity. The Father contemplates His work: There is My creature! ...The Son, the price of His Blood: the beauty of an object is shown by the price it has cost. ...The Holy Spirit dwells in it, as in a temple.

We also know the value of our soul by the efforts the devil makes to ruin it. Hell is leagued against it—Heaven for it. Oh, how great it must be! In order to have an idea of our dignity, we must often think of Heaven, Calvary, and Hell. If we could understand what it is to be the child of God, we could not do evil—we should be like angels on earth. To be children of God, oh, what a dignity!

It is a beautiful thing to have a heart, and, little as it is, to be able to make use of it in loving God. How shameful it is that man should descend so low, when God has placed him so high! When the angels had revolted against God, this God who is so good, seeing that they could no longer enjoy the happiness for which He had created them, made man, and this little world that we see to nourish his body. But his soul required to be nourished also; and as nothing created can feed the soul, which is a spirit, God willed to give Himself for its Food. But the great misfortune is that we neglect to have recourse to this divine Food, in crossing the desert of this life. Like people who die of hunger within sight of a well-provided table, there are some who remain fifty, sixty years, without feeding their souls.

Oh, if Christians could understand the language of Our Lord, who says to them, "Notwithstanding thy misery, I wish to see near Me that beautiful soul which I created for Myself. I made it so great, that nothing can fill it but Myself. I made it so pure, that nothing but My Body can nourish it."

Our Lord has always distinguished pure souls.

Look at St. John, the well-beloved disciple, who reposed upon His breast. St. Catherine was pure, and she was often transported into Paradise. When she died, angels took up her body, and carried it to Mount Sinai, where Moses had received the Commandments of the law. God has shown by this prodigy that a soul is so agreeable to Him, that it deserves that even the body which has participated in its purity should be buried by angels.

God contemplates a pure soul with love; He grants it all it desires. How could He refuse anything to a soul that lives only for Him, by Him, and in Him? It seeks God, and He shows Himself to it; it calls Him, and God comes; it is one with Him; it captivates His will. A pure soul is all-powerful with the gracious Heart of Our Lord. A pure soul with God is like a child with its mother. It caresses her, it embraces her, and its mother returns its caresses and embraces.

CHAPTER 7

Catechism on the Sanctification of Sunday

YOU LABOR, you labor, my children; but what you earn ruins your body and your soul. If one ask those who work on Sunday, "What have you been doing?" they might answer, "I have been selling my soul to the devil, crucifying Our Lord, and renouncing my Baptism. I am going to Hell; I shall have to weep for all eternity in vain." When I see people driving carts on Sunday, I think I see them carrying their souls to Hell.

Oh, how mistaken in his calculations is he who labors hard on Sunday, thinking that he will earn more money or do more work! Can two or three shillings ever make up for the harm he does himself by violating the law of the good God? You imagine that everything depends on your working; but there comes an illness, an accident. . . . so little is required! a tempest, a hailstorm, a frost. The good God holds everything in His hand; He can avenge Himself when He will, and as He will; the means are not wanting to Him. Is He not always the strongest? Must not He be the master in the end?

There was once a woman who came to her

priest to ask leave to get in her hay on Sunday. "But," said the priest, "it is not necessary; your hay will run no risk." The woman insisted, saying, "Then you want me to let my crop be lost?" She herself died that very evening; she was more in danger than her crop of hay. "Labor not for the meat which perisheth, but for that which endureth unto life everlasting." [*Jn.* 6:27].

What will remain to you of your Sunday work? You leave the earth just as it is; when you go away, you carry nothing with you. Ah! when we are attached to the earth, we are not willing to go! Our first end is to go to God; we are on the earth for no other purpose. My brethren, we should die on Sunday, and rise again on Monday.

Sunday is the property of our good God; it is His own day, the Lord's day. He made all the days of the week: He might have kept them all; He has given you six, and has reserved only the seventh for Himself. What right have you to meddle with what does not belong to you? You know very well that stolen goods never bring any profit. Nor will the day that you steal from Our Lord profit you either. I know two very certain ways of becoming poor: they are working on Sunday and taking other people's property.

Chapter 8

Catechism on Prayer

SEE MY children; the treasure of a Christian is not on the earth, it is in Heaven. Well, our thoughts ought to be where our treasure is. Man has a beautiful office, that of praying and loving. You pray, you love—that is the happiness of man upon the earth. Prayer is nothing else than union with God. When our heart is pure and united to God, we feel within ourselves a joy, a sweetness that inebriates, a light that dazzles us. In this intimate union God and the soul are like two pieces of wax melted together; they cannot be separated. This union of God with His little creature is a most beautiful thing. It is a happiness that we cannot understand.

We have not deserved to pray; but God, in His goodness, has permitted us to speak to Him. Our prayer is an incense which He receives with extreme pleasure. My children, your heart is poor and narrow; but prayer enlarges it, and renders it capable of loving God. Prayer is a foretaste of Heaven, an overflow of paradise. It never leaves us without sweetness. It is like honey descending into the soul and sweetening everything. Troubles melt away before a fervent prayer like snow

before the sun. Prayer makes time pass away very
quickly, and so pleasantly that one does not perceive how it passes. Do you know, when I was
running up and down the country, at the time
that almost all the poor priests were ill, I was
praying to the good God all along the road. I
assure you, the time did not seem long to me.

We see some persons who lose themselves in
prayer like a fish in the water, because they are
all for God. There is not division in their heart.
Oh, how I love those generous souls! St. Francis
of Assisi and St. Colette saw Our Lord and spoke
to Him as we talk to each other. While we, how
often we come to church without knowing what
we come for, or what we are going to ask! And
yet, when we go to one's house, we know very
well what we are going for. Some people seem
to say to God, "I am going to say two words to
Thee, to get rid of Thee." I often think that when
we come to adore Our Lord, we should obtain
all we wish, if we would ask it with very lively
faith, and a very pure heart. But, alas! we have
no faith, no hope, no desire, no love!

There are two cries in man, the cry of the angel
and the cry of the beast. The cry of the angel
is prayer; the cry of the beast is sin. Those who
do not pray, stoop towards the earth, like a mole
trying to make a hole to hide itself in. They are
all earthly, all brutish, and think of nothing but
temporal things, . . . like that miser who was
receiving the last Sacraments the other day; when
they gave him a silver crucifix to kiss, he said,

"That cross weighs full ten ounces." If there could be one day without worship, it would no longer be Heaven; and if the poor lost souls, notwithstanding their sufferings, could worship, there would be no more Hell. Alas! they had a heart to love God with, a tongue to bless Him with; that was their destiny. And now they are condemned to curse Him through all eternity. If they could hope that they would once pray only for one minute, they would watch for that minute with such impatience that it would lessen their torments.

"Our Father who art in Heaven!" Oh, how beautiful it is, my children, to have a father in Heaven! "Thy kingdom come." If I make the good God reign in my heart, He will make me reign with Him in His glory. "Thy will be done." There is nothing so sweet, and nothing so perfect, as to do the will of God. In order to do things well, we must do them as God wills, in all conformity with His designs. "Give us this day our daily bread." We are composed of two parts, the soul and the body. We ask the good God to feed our poor body, and He answers by making the earth produce all that is necessary for our support.
...But we ask Him to feed our soul, which is the best part of ourselves; and the earth is too small to furnish enough to satisfy it; it hungers for God, and nothing but God can satiate it. Therefore the good God thought He did not do too much, in dwelling upon the earth and assuming a body, in order that this Body might

become the Food of our souls. "My Flesh," said Our Lord, "is meat indeed. . . .The bread that I will give is my Flesh, for the life of the world."

The bread of souls is in the tabernacle. The tabernacle is the storehouse of Christians. . . .Oh, how beautiful it is, my children! When the priest presents the Host, and shows it to you, your soul may say, "There is my food." O my children, we are too happy! . . .We shall never comprehend it till we are in Heaven. What a pity that is!

CHAPTER 9

Catechism on the Priesthood

M Y CHILDREN, we have come to the Sacrament of Orders. It is a Sacrament which seems to relate to no one among you, and which yet relates to everyone. This Sacrament raises man up to God. What is a priest! A man who holds the place of God—a man who is invested with all the powers of God. "Go," said Our Lord to the priest; "as My Father sent Me, I send you. All power has been given Me in Heaven and on earth. Go then, teach all nations. . . . He who listens to you, listens to Me; he who despises you despises Me." When the priest remits sins, he does not say, "God pardons you"; he says, "I absolve you." At the Consecration, he does not say, "This is the Body of Our Lord;" he says, "This is My Body."

St. Bernard tells us that everything has come to us through Mary; and we may also say that everything has come to us through the priest; yes, all happiness, all graces, all heavenly gifts. If we had not the Sacrament of Orders, we should not have Our Lord. Who placed Him there, in that tabernacle? It was the priest. Who was it that received your soul, on its entrance into life? The priest. Who nourishes it, to give it strength to make its pilgrimage? The priest. Who will prepare it to appear before God, by washing that soul, for the last time, in the blood of Jesus Christ? The priest—always the priest. And if that soul comes to the point of death, who will raise it up, who will restore it to calmness and peace? Again the priest. You cannot recall one single blessing from God without finding, side by side with this recollection, the image of the priest.

Go to confession to the Blessed Virgin, or to an angel; will they absolve you? No. Will they give you the Body and Blood of Our Lord? No. The Holy Virgin cannot make her Divine Son descend into the Host. You might have two hundred angels there, but they could not absolve you. A priest, however simple he may be, can do it; he can say to you, "Go in peace; I pardon you." Oh, how great is a priest! The priest will not understand the greatness of his office till he is in Heaven. If he understood it on earth, he would die, not of fear, but of love. The other benefits of God would be of no avail to us without the priest. What would be the use of a house full of gold, if you had nobody to open you the door! The priest has the key of the heavenly treasures; it is he who opens the door; he is the steward of the good God, the distributor of His wealth. Without the priest, the Death and Passion of Our Lord would be of no avail. Look at the heathens: what has it availed them that Our Lord has died? Alas! they can have no share in the blessings of

Redemption, while they have no priests to apply His Blood to their souls!

The priest is not a priest for himself; he does not give himself absolution; he does not administer the Sacraments to himself. He is not for himself, he is for you. After God, the priest is everything. Leave a parish twenty years without priests; they will worship beasts. If the missionary Father and I were to go away, you would say, "What can we do in this church? there is no Mass; Our Lord is no longer there: we may as well pray at home." When people wish to destroy religion, they begin by attacking the priest, because where there is no longer any priest there is no sacrifice, and where there is no longer any sacrifice there is no religion.

When the bell calls you to church, if you were asked, "Where are you going?" you might answer, "I am going to feed my soul." If someone were to ask you, pointing to the tabernacle, "What is that golden door?" "That is our storehouse, where the true Food of our souls is kept." "Who has the key? Who lays in the provisions? Who makes ready the feast, and who serves the table?" "The priest." "And what is the Food?" "The precious Body and Blood of Our Lord." O God! O God! how Thou hast loved us! See the power of the priest; out of a piece of bread the word of a priest makes a God. It is more than creating the world. . . . Someone said, "Does St. Philomena, then, obey the Curé of Ars?" Indeed, she may well obey him, since God obeys him.

If I were to meet a priest and an angel, I should salute the priest before I saluted the angel. The latter is the friend of God; but the priest holds His place. St. Teresa kissed the ground where a priest had passed. When you see a priest, you should say, "There is he who made me a child of God, and opened Heaven to me by holy Baptism; he who purified me after I had sinned; who gives nourishment to my soul." At the sight of a church tower, you may say, "What is there in that place?" "The Body of Our Lord." "Why is He there?" "Because a priest has been there, and has said holy Mass."

What joy did the Apostles feel after the Resurrection of Our Lord, at seeing the Master whom they had loved so much! The priest must feel the same joy, at seeing Our Lord whom he holds in his hands. Great value is attached to objects which have been laid in the drinking cup of the Blessed Virgin and of the Child Jesus, at Loretto. But the fingers of the priest, that have touched the adorable Flesh of Jesus Christ, that have been plunged into the chalice which contained His Blood, into the pyx where His Body has lain, are they not still more precious? The priesthood is the love of the Heart of Jesus. When you see the priest, think of Our Lord Jesus Christ.

CHAPTER 10

Catechism on the Holy Sacrifice
of the Mass

ALL GOOD WORKS together are not of equal
value with the sacrifice of the Mass, because
they are the works of men, and the holy Mass
is the work of God. Martyrdom is nothing in comparison; it is the sacrifice that man makes of his
life to God; the Mass is the sacrifice that God
makes to man of His Body and of His Blood. Oh,
how great is a priest! if he understood himself
he would die. . . . God obeys him; he speaks two
words, and Our Lord comes down from Heaven
at his voice, and shuts Himself up in a little Host.
God looks upon the altar. "That is My well-
beloved Son," He says, "in whom I am well-
pleased." He can refuse nothing to the merits of
the offering of this Victim. If we had faith, we
should see God hidden in the priest like a light
behind a glass, like wine mingled with water.

After the Consecration, when I hold in my
hands the most holy Body of Our Lord, and when
I am in discouragement, seeing myself worthy of
nothing but Hell, I say to myself, "Ah, if I could
at least take Him with me! Hell would be sweet
with Him; I could be content to remain suffering

there for all eternity, if we were together. But then there would be no more Hell; the flames of love would extinguish those of justice." How beautiful it is. After the Consecration, the good God is there as He is in Heaven. If man well understood this mystery, he would die of love. God spares us because of our weakness. A priest once, after the Consecration, had some little doubt whether his few words could have made Our Lord descend upon the Altar; at the same moment he saw the Host all red, and the corporal tinged with blood.

If someone said to us, "At such an hour a dead person is to be raised to life," we should run very quickly to see it. But is not the Consecration, which changes bread and wine into the Body and Blood of God, a much greater miracle than to raise a dead person to life? We ought always to devote at least a quarter of an hour to preparing ourselves to hear Mass well; we ought to annihilate ourselves before God, after the example of His profound annihilation in the Sacrament of the Eucharist; and we should make our examination of conscience, for we must be in a state of grace to be able to assist properly at Mass. If we knew the value of the holy Sacrifice of the Mass, or rather if we had faith, we should be much more zealous to assist at it.

My children, you remember the story I have told you already of that holy priest who was praying for his friend; God had, it appears, made known to him that he was in Purgatory; it came into his mind that he could do nothing better than to offer the holy Sacrifice of the Mass for his soul. When he came to the moment of Consecration, he took the Host in his hands and said, "O Holy and Eternal Father, let us make an exchange. Thou hast the soul of my friend who is in Purgatory, and I have the Body of Thy Son, Who is in my hands; well, do Thou deliver my friend, and I offer Thee Thy Son, with all the merits of His Death and Passion." In fact, at the moment of the elevation, he saw the soul of his friend rising to Heaven, all radiant with glory. Well, my children, when we want to obtain anything from the good God, let us do the same; after Holy Communion, let us offer Him His wellbeloved Son, with all the merits of His death and His Passion. He will not be able to refuse us anything.

CHAPTER 11

Catechism on the Real Presence

OUR LORD is hidden there, waiting for us to come and visit Him, and make our request to Him. See how good He is! He accommodates Himself to our weakness. In Heaven, where we shall be glorious and triumphant, we shall see him in all His glory. If He had presented Himself before us in that glory now, we should not have dared to approach Him; but He hides Himself, like a person in a prison, who might say to us, "You do not see me, but that is no matter; ask of me all you wish and I will grant it." He is there in the Sacrament of His love, sighing and interceding incessantly with His Father for sinners. To what outrages does He not expose Himself, that He may remain in the midst of us! He is there to console us; and therefore we ought often to visit Him. How pleasing to Him is the short quarter of an hour that we steal from our occupations, from something of no use, to come and pray to Him, to visit Him, to console Him for all the outrages He receives! When He sees pure souls coming eagerly to Him, He smiles upon them. They come with that simplicity which pleases Him so much, to ask His pardon for all sinners, for the outrages of so many ungrateful men. What happiness do we not feel in the presence of God, when we find ourselves alone at His feet before the holy tabernacles! "Come, my soul, redouble thy fervor; thou art alone adoring thy God. His eyes rest upon thee alone." This good Saviour is so full of love for us that He seeks us out everywhere.

Ah! if we had the eyes of angels with which to see Our Lord Jesus Christ, who is here present on this altar, and who is looking at us, how we should love Him! We should never more wish to part from Him. We should wish to remain always at His feet; it would be a foretaste of Heaven: all else would become insipid to us. But see, it is faith we want. We are poor blind people; we have a mist before our eyes. Faith alone can dispel this mist. Presently, my children, when I shall hold Our Lord in my hands, when the good God blesses you, ask Him then to open the eyes of your heart; say to Him like the blind man of Jericho, "O Lord, make me to see!" If you say to Him sincerely, "Make me to see!" you will certainly obtain what you desire, because He wishes nothing but your happiness. He has His hands full of graces, seeking to whom to distribute them; alas! and no one will have them. . . .Oh, indifference! Oh, ingratitude! My children, we are most unhappy that we do not understand these things! We shall understand them well one day; but it will then be too late!

Our Lord is there as a Victim; and a prayer

that is very pleasing to God is to ask the Blessed Virgin to offer to the Eternal Father her Divine Son, all bleeding, all torn, for the conversion of sinners; it is the best prayer we can make, since, indeed, all prayers are made in the name and through the merits of Jesus Christ. We must also thank God for all those indulgences that purify us from our sins...but we pay no attention to them. We tread upon indulgences, one might say, as we tread upon the sheaves of corn after the harvest. See, there are seven years and seven quarantines for hearing the catechism, three hundred days for reciting the Litany of the Blessed Virgin, the Salve Regina, the Angelus. In short, the good God multiplies His graces upon us; and how sorry we shall be at the end of our lives that we did not profit by them!

When we are before the Blessed Sacrament, instead of looking about, let us shut our eyes and our mouth; let us open our heart: our good God will open His; we shall go to Him, He will come to us, the one to ask, the other to receive; it will be like a breath from one to the other. What sweetness do we not find in forgetting ourselves in order to seek God! The saints lost sight of themselves that they might see nothing but God, and labor for Him alone; they forgot all created objects in order to find Him alone. This is the way to reach Heaven.

CHAPTER 12

Catechism on Communion

TO SUSTAIN the soul in the pilgrimage of
life, God looked over creation, and found
nothing that was worthy of it. He then turned
to Himself, and resolved to give Himself. O my
soul, how great thou art, since nothing less than
God can satisfy thee! The food of the soul is the
Body and Blood of God! Oh, admirable Food!
If we considered it, it would make us lose ourselves in that abyss of love for all eternity! How
happy are the pure souls that have the happiness
of being united to Our Lord by Communion! They
will shine like beautiful diamonds in Heaven, because God will be seen in them.

Our Lord has said, Whatever you shall ask the
Father in My name, He will give it you. We should
never have thought of asking of God His own Son.
But God has done what man could not have imagined. What man cannot express nor conceive,
and what he never would have dared to desire,
God in His love has said, has conceived, and has
executed. Should we ever have dared to ask of
God to put His Son to death for us, to give us
His Flesh to eat and His Blood to drink? If all
this were not true, then man might have imagined

things that God cannot do; he would have gone further than God in inventions of love! That is impossible. Without the Holy Eucharist there would be no happiness in this world; life would be insupportable. When we receive Holy Communion, we receive our joy and our happiness. The good God, wishing to give Himself to us in the Sacrament of His love, gave us a vast and great desire, which He alone can satisfy. In the presence of this beautiful Sacrament, we are like a person dying of thirst by the side of a river—he would only need to bend his head; like a person still remaining poor, close to a great treasure—he need only stretch out his hand. He who communicates loses himself in God like a drop of water in the ocean. They can no more be separated.

At the Day of Judgment we shall see the Flesh of Our Lord shine through the glorified body of those who have received Him worthily on earth, as we see gold shine in copper, or silver in lead. When we have just communicated, if we were asked, "What are you carrying away to your home?" we might answer, "I am carrying away Heaven." A saint said that we were Christ-bearers. It is very true; but we have not enough faith. We do not comprehend our dignity. When we leave the holy banquet, we are as happy as the Wise Men would have been, if they could have carried away the Infant Jesus. Take a vessel full of liquor, and cork it well—you will keep the liquor as long as you please. So if you were to keep Our Lord well and recollectedly, after

Communion, you would long feel that devouring fire which would inspire your heart with an inclination to good and a repugnance to evil. When we have the good God in our heart, it ought to be very burning. The heart of the disciples of Emmaus burnt within them from merely listening to His voice.

I do not like people to begin to read directly when they come from the holy table. Oh no! what is the use of the words of men when God is speaking? We must do as one who is very curious, and listens at the door. We must listen to all that God says at the door of our heart. When you have received Our Lord, you feel your soul purified, because it bathes itself in the love of God. When we go to Holy Communion, we feel something extraordinary, a comfort which pervades the whole body, and penetrates to the extremities. What is this comfort? It is Our Lord, who communicates Himself to all parts of our bodies, and makes them thrill. We are obliged to say, like St. John, "It is the Lord!" Those who feel absolutely nothing are very much to be pitied.

CHAPTER 13

Catechism on Frequent Communion

MY CHILDREN, all beings in creation require to be fed, that they may live; for this purpose God has made trees and plants grow; it is a well-served table, to which all animals come and take the food which suits each one. But the soul also must be fed. Where, then, is its food? My brethren, the food of the soul is God. Ah! what a beautiful thought! The soul can feed on nothing but God. Only God can suffice for it; only God can fill it; only God can satiate its hunger; it absolutely requires its God! There is in all houses a place where the provisions of the family are kept; it is the store-room. The church is the home of souls; it is the house belonging to us, who are Christians. Well, in this house there is a store-room. Do you see the tabernacle? If the souls of Christians were asked, "What is that?" your souls would answer, "It is the store-room."

There is nothing so great, my children, as the Eucharist! Put all the good works in the world against one good Communion; they will be like a grain of dust beside a mountain. Make a prayer when you have the good God in your heart; the

46

good God will not be able to refuse you anything, if you offer Him His Son, and the merits of His holy death and Passion. My children, if we understood the value of Holy Communion, we should avoid the least faults, that we might have the happiness of making it oftener. We should keep our souls always pure in the eyes of God. My children, I suppose that you have been to confession today, and you will watch over yourselves; you will be happy in the thought that tomorrow you will have the joy of receiving the good God into your heart. Neither can you offend the good God tomorrow; your soul will be all embalmed with the precious Blood of Our Lord. Oh, beautiful life!

O my children, how beautiful will a soul be in eternity that has worthily and often received the good God! The Body of Our Lord will shine through our body, His adorable Blood through our blood; our soul will be united to the Soul of Our Lord during all eternity. There it will enjoy pure and perfect happiness. My children, when the soul of a Christian who has received Our Lord enters paradise, it augments the joy of Heaven. The Angels and the Queen of Angels come to meet it, because they recognize the Son of God in that soul. Then will that soul be rewarded for the pains and sacrifices it will have endured in its life on earth. My children, we know when a soul has worthily received the Sacrament of the Eucharist, it is so drowned in love, so penetrated and changed, that it is no longer to be recognized in its words or its actions. . . . It is humble, it is gentle, it is

mortified, charitable, and modest; it is at peace
with everyone. It is a soul capable of the greatest
sacrifices; in short, you would not know it again.

Go, then, to Communion, my children; go to
Jesus with love and confidence; go and live upon
Him, in order to live for Him! Do not say that
you have too much to do. Has not the Divine Saviour said, "Come to Me, all you that labour and
are burdened, and I will refresh you"? Can you
resist an invitation so full of love and tenderness?
Do not say that you are not worthy of it. It is
true, you are not worthy of it; but you are in need
of it. If Our Lord had regarded our worthiness,
He would never have instituted His beautiful
Sacrament of love: for no one in the world is worthy of it, neither the saints, nor the angels, nor
the archangels, nor the Blessed Virgin; but He had
in view our needs, and we are all in need of it.
Do not say that you are sinners, that you are too
miserable, and for that reason you do not dare
to approach it. I would as soon hear you say that
you are very ill, and therefore you will not take
any remedy, nor send for the physician.

All the prayers of the Mass are a preparation
for Communion; and all the life of a Christian
ought to be a preparation for that great action.
We ought to labor to deserve to receive Our Lord
every day. How humbled we ought to feel when
we see others going to the holy table, and we
remain motionless in our place! How happy is
a guardian angel who leads a beautiful soul to
the holy table! In the primitive Church they

communicated every day. When Christians had grown cold, they substituted blessed bread for the Body of Our Lord; this is both a consolation and a humiliation. It is indeed blessed bread; but it is not the Body and Blood of Our Lord!

There are some who make a spiritual communion every day with blessed bread. If we are deprived of Sacramental Communion, let us replace it, as far as we can, by spiritual communion, which we can make every moment; for we ought to have always a burning desire to receive the good God. Communion is to the soul like blowing a fire that is beginning to go out, but that has still plenty of hot embers; we blow, and the fire burns again. After the reception of the Sacraments, when we feel ourselves slacken in the love of God, let us have recourse at once to spiritual communion. When we cannot come to church, let us turn towards the tabernacle: a wall cannot separate us from the good God; let us say five *Patres* and five *Aves* to make a spiritual communion. We can receive the good God only once a day; a soul on fire with love supplies for this by the desire to receive Him every moment. O man, how great thou art! fed with the Body and Blood of a God! Oh, how sweet a life is this life of union with the good God! It is Heaven upon earth; there are no more troubles, no more crosses! When you have the happiness of having received the good God, you feel a joy, a sweetness in your heart for some moments. Pure souls feel it always, and in this union consists their strength and their happiness.

CHAPTER 14

Catechism on Sin

SIN IS the executioner of the good God, and the assassin of the soul. It snatches us away from Heaven to precipitate us into Hell. And we love it! What folly! If we thought seriously about it, we should have such a lively horror of sin that we could not commit it. O my children, how ungrateful we are! The good God wishes to make us happy; that is very certain; He gave us His Law for no other end. The Law of God is great; it is broad. King David said that he found his delight in it, and that it was a treasure more precious to him than the greatest riches. He said also that he walked at large, because he had sought after the Commandments of the Lord. The good God wishes, then, to make us happy, and we do not wish to be so. We turn away from Him, and give ourselves to the devil! We fly from our Friend, and we seek after our murderer! We commit sin; we plunge ourselves into the mire. Once sunk in this mire, we know not how to get out. If our fortune were in the case, we should soon find out how to get out of the difficulty; but because it only concerns our soul, we stay where we are.

We come to confession quite preoccupied with

50

the shame that we shall feel. We accuse ourselves *by steam*. It is said that many confess, and few are converted. I believe it is so, my children, because few confess with tears of repentance. See, the misfortune is, that people do not reflect. If one said to those who work on Sundays, to a young person who had been dancing for two or three hours, to a man coming out of an alehouse drunk, "What have you been doing? You have been crucifying Our Lord!" they would be quite astonished, because they do not think of it. My children, if we thought of it, we should be seized with horror; it would be impossible for us to do evil. For what has the good God done to us that we should grieve Him thus, and put Him to death afresh—Him, who has redeemed us from Hell? It would be well if all sinners, when they are going to their guilty pleasures, could, like St. Peter, meet Our Lord on the way, who would say to them, "I am going to that place where thou art going thyself, to be there crucified afresh." Perhaps that might make them reflect.

The saints understood how great an outrage sin is against God. Some of them passed their lives in weeping for their sins. St. Peter wept all his life; he was still weeping at his death. St. Bernard used to say, "Lord! Lord! it is I who fastened Thee to the Cross!" By sin we despise the good God, we crucify the good God! What a pity it is to lose our souls, which have cost Our Lord so many sufferings! What harm has Our Lord done us, that we should treat Him so? If the poor lost souls could come back to the earth! if they were in our place! Oh, how senseless we are! the good God calls us to Him, and we fly from Him! He wishes to make us happy, and we will not have His happiness. He commands us to love Him, and we give our hearts to the devil. We employ in ruining ourselves the time He gives us to save our souls. We make war upon Him with the means He gave us to serve Him.

When we offend the good God, if we were to look at our crucifix, we should hear Our Lord saying to us in the depths of our soul, "Wilt thou too, then, take the side of My enemies? Wilt thou crucify Me afresh?" Cast your eyes on Our Lord fastened to the Cross, and say to yourself, "That is what it cost my Saviour to repair the injury my sins have done to God!" A God coming down to earth to be the victim of our sins, a God suffering, a God dying, a God enduring every torment, because He would bear the weight of our crimes! At the sight of the Cross, let us understand the malice of sin, and the hatred we ought to feel for it. Let us enter into ourselves; let us see what we can do to make amends for our poor life.

"What a pity it is!" the good God will say to us at our death; "why hast thou offended Me— Me, who loved thee so much?" To offend the good God, who has never done us anything but good; to please the devil, who can never do us anything but evil! What folly! Is it not real folly to choose to make ourselves worthy of Hell by attaching ourselves to the devil, when we might taste the joys of Heaven, even in this life, by uniting ourselves to God by love? One cannot understand this folly; it cannot be enough lamented. Poor sinners seem as if they could not wait for the sentence which will condemn them to the society of the devils; they condemn themselves to it. There is a sort of foretaste in this life of Paradise, of Hell, and of Purgatory. Purgatory is in those souls that are not dead to themselves; Hell is in the heart of the impious; Paradise in that of the perfect, who are closely united to Our Lord.

He who lives in sin takes up the habits and the appearance of the beasts. The beast, which has not reason, knows nothing but its appetites. So the man who makes himself like the beasts loses his reason, and lets himself be guided by the inclinations of his body. He takes his pleasure in good eating and drinking, and in enjoying the vanities of the world, which pass away like the wind. I pity the poor wretches who run after that wind; they gain very little, they give a great deal for very little profit—they give their eternity for the miserable smoke of the world.

My children, how sad it is! when a soul is in a state of sin, it may die in that state; and even now, whatever it can do is without merit before God. That is the reason why the devil is so pleased when a soul is in sin, and perseveres in it, because he thinks that it is working for him, and if it were to die he would have possession of it. When we are in sin, our soul is all diseased, all rotten; it is pitiful. The thought that the good

God sees it ought to make it enter into itself. And then, what pleasure is there in sin? None at all. We have frightful dreams that the devil is carrying us away, that we are falling over precipices. Put yourself on good terms with God; have recourse to the Sacrament of Penance; you will sleep as quietly as an angel. You will be glad to waken in the night, to pray to God; you will have nothing but thanksgivings on your lips; you will rise towards Heaven with great facility, as an eagle soars through the air.

See, my children, how sin degrades man; of an angel created to love God, it makes a demon who will curse Him for eternity. Ah! if Adam, our first father, had not sinned, and if we did not sin every day, how happy we should be! we should be as happy as the saints in Heaven. There would be no more unhappy people on the earth. Oh, how beautiful it would be! In fact, my children, it is sin that brings upon us all calamities, all scourges, war, famine, pestilence, earthquakes, fires, frost, hail, storms—all that afflicts us, all that makes us miserable. See, my children, a person who is in a state of sin is always sad. Whatever he does, he is weary and disgusted with everything; while he who is at peace with God is always happy, always joyous. . . .Oh, beautiful life! Oh, beautiful death!

My children, we are afraid of death; I can well believe it. It is sin that makes us afraid of death; it is sin that renders death frightful, formidable; it is sin that terrifies the wicked at the hour of the fearful passage. Alas! O God! there is reason enough to be terrified, to think that one is accursed—accursed of God! It makes one tremble. Accursed of God! and why? for what do men expose themselves to be accursed of God? For a blasphemy, for a bad thought, for a bottle of wine, for two minutes of pleasure! For two minutes of pleasure to lose God, one's soul, Heaven forever! We shall see going up to Heaven, in body and soul, that father, that mother, that sister, that neighbor, who were here with us, with whom we have lived, but whom we have not imitated; while we shall go down body and soul to burn in Hell. The devils will rush to overwhelm us. All the devils whose advice we followed will come to torment us.

My children, if you saw a man prepare a great pile of wood, heaping up fagots one upon another, and when you asked him what he was doing, he were to answer you, "I am preparing the fire that is to burn me," what would you think? And if you saw this same man set fire to the pile, and when it was lighted throw himself upon it, what would you say? This is what we do when we commit sin. It is not God who casts us into Hell; we cast ourselves into it by our sins. The lost souls will say, "I have lost God, my soul, and Heaven; it is through my fault, through my fault, through my most grievous fault!" He will raise himself out of the fire only to fall back into it. He will always feel the desire of rising because he was created for God, the greatest, the highest of beings, the Most High...as a bird shut up in a room flies to the ceiling, and falls down again, the justice of God is the ceiling which keeps down the lost.

There is no need to prove the existence of Hell. Our Lord Himself speaks of it, when He relates the history of the wicked rich man who cried out, "Lazarus! Lazarus!" We know very well that there is a Hell, but we live as if there were not; we sell our souls for a few pieces of money. We put off our conversion till the hour of death; but who can assure us that we shall have time or strength at that formidable moment, which has been feared by all the saints—when Hell will gather itself up for a last assault upon us, seeing that it is the decisive moment? There are many people who lose the faith, and never see Hell till they enter it. The Sacraments are administered to them; but ask them if they have committed such a sin, and they will answer you, "Oh! settle that as you please."

Some people offend the good God every moment; their heart is an anthill of sins: it is like a spoilt piece of meat, half-eaten by worms. ...No, indeed; if sinners were to think of eternity—of that terrible forever—they would be converted instantly.

CHAPTER 15

Catechism on Pride

PRIDE IS that accursed sin which drove the angels out of paradise, and hurled them into Hell. This sin began with the world. See, my children, we sin by pride in many ways. A person may be proud in his clothes, in his language, in his gestures, even in his manner of walking. Some persons, when they are in the streets, walk along proudly, and seem to say to the people they meet, "Look how tall, how upright I am, how well I walk!" Others, when they have done any good action, are never tired of talking of it; and if they fail in anything, they are miserable because they think people will have a bad opinion of them...others are sorry to be seen with the poor, if they meet with anybody of consequence; they are always seeking the company of the rich...if by chance, they are noticed by the great people of the world, they boast and are vain of it. Others take pride in speaking. If they go to see rich people, they consider what they are going to say, they study fine language; and if they make a mistake of a word, they are very much vexed, because they are afraid of being laughed at. But, my children, with a humble person it is not so...whether

57

he is laughed at or esteemed, or praised, or
blamed, whether he is honored or despised,
whether people pay attention to him or pass him
by, it is all the same to him.

My children, there are again people who give
great alms, that they may be well thought of—
that will not do! These people will reap no fruit
from their good works. On the contrary, their alms
will turn into sins. We put pride into everything
like salt. We like to see that our good works are
known. If our virtues are seen, we are pleased;
if our faults are perceived, we are sad. I remark
that in a great many people; if one says anything
to them, it disturbs them, it annoys them. The
saints were not like that—they were vexed if their
virtues were known, and pleased that their imperfections should be seen. A proud person thinks
everything he does is well done; he wants to dom-
ineer over all those who have to do with him;
he is always right, he always thinks his own opinion better than that of others. That will not do!
A humble and well-taught person, if he is asked
his opinion, gives it at once, and then lets others
speak. Whether they are right, or whether they
are wrong, he says nothing more.

When St. Aloysius Gonzaga was a student, he
never sought to excuse himself when he was
reproached with anything; he said what he
thought, and troubled himself no further about
what others might think; if he was wrong, he
was wrong; if he was right, he said to himself,
"I have certainly been wrong some other time."

My children, the saints were so completely dead to themselves, that they cared very little whether others agreed with them. People in the world say, "Oh, the saints were simpletons!" Yes, they were simpletons in worldly things; but in the things of God they were very wise. They understood nothing about worldly matters, to be sure, because they thought them of so little importance, that they paid no attention to them.

CHAPTER 16

Catechism on Impurity

THAT WE MAY understand how horrible and detestable is this sin, which the demons make us commit, but which they do not commit themselves, we must consider what a Christian is. A Christian, created in the image of God, redeemed by the Blood of a God! a Christian, the child of God, the brother of a God, the heir of a God! a Christian, whose body is the temple of the Holy Ghost; that is what sin dishonors. We are created to reign one day in Heaven, and if we have the misfortune to commit this sin, we become the den of the devils. Our Lord said that nothing impure should enter into His kingdom. Indeed, how could a soul that has rolled itself in this filth go to appear before so pure and so holy a God?

We are all like little mirrors, in which God contemplates Himself. How can you expect that God should recognize His likeness in an impure soul? There are some souls so dead, so *rotten*, that they lie in their defilement without perceiving it, and can no longer clear themselves from it; everything leads them to evil, everything reminds them of evil, even the most holy things; they always have these abominations before their eyes; like the unclean animal that is accustomed to live in filth, that is happy in it, that rolls itself and goes to sleep in it, that grunts in the mud; these persons are an object of horror in the eyes of God and of the holy angels. See, my children, Our Lord was crowned with thorns to expiate our sins of pride; but for this accursed sin, He was scourged and torn to pieces, since He said Himself that after his flagellation all His bones might be counted.

O my children, if there were not some pure souls here and there, to make amends to the good God, and disarm His justice, you would see how we should be punished! For now, this crime is so common in the world, that it is enough to make one tremble. One may say, my children, that Hell vomits forth its abominations upon the earth, as the chimneys of the steam engine vomit forth smoke. The devil does all he can to defile our soul, and yet our soul is everything...our body is only a heap of corruption: go to the cemetery to see what you love, when you love your body. As I have often told you, there is nothing so vile as the impure soul. There was once a saint, who had asked the good God to show him one; and he saw that poor soul like a dead beast that has been dragged through the streets in the hot sun for a week.

By only looking at a person, we know if he is pure. His eyes have an air of candor and modesty which leads you to the good God. Some people, on the contrary, look quite inflamed with passion...Satan places himself in their eyes to make others fall and to lead them to evil. Those who have lost their purity are like a piece of cloth stained with oil; you may wash it and dry it, and the stain always appears again: so it requires a miracle to cleanse the impure soul.

Catechism on Confession

MY CHILDREN, as soon as ever you have a little spot upon your soul, you must do like a person who has a fine globe of glass, which he keeps very carefully. If this globe has a little dust on it, he wipes it with a sponge the moment he perceives it, and there is the globe clear and brilliant. In the same way, as soon as you perceive a little stain on your soul, take some holy water with respect, do one of those good works to which the remission of venial sins is attached— an alms, a genuflection to the Blessed Sacrament, hearing a Mass. My children, it is like a person who has a slight illness; he need not go and see a doctor, he may cure himself without. If he has a headache, he need only go to bed; if he is hungry, he has only to eat. But if it is a serious illness, if it is a dangerous wound, he must have the doctor; after the doctor come the remedies. In the same way, when we have fallen into any grievous sin, we must have recourse to the doctor, that is the priest; and to the remedy, that is confession.

My children, we cannot comprehend the goodness of God towards us in instituting this great

Sacrament of Penance. If we had had a favor to ask of Our Lord, we should never have thought of asking Him that. But He foresaw our frailty and our inconstancy in well-doing, and His love induced Him to do what we should not have dared to ask. If one said to those poor lost souls that have been so long in Hell, "We are going to place a priest at the gate of Hell: all those who wish to confess have only to go out," do you think, my children, that a single one would remain? The most guilty would not be afraid of telling their sins, nor even of telling them before all the world. Oh, how soon Hell would be a desert, and how Heaven would be peopled! Well, we have the time and the means, which those poor lost souls have not. And I am quite sure that those wretched ones say in Hell, "O accursed priest! if I had never known you, I should not be so guilty!"

It is a beautiful thought, my children, that we have a Sacrament which heals the wounds of our soul! But we must receive it with good dispositions. Otherwise we make new wounds upon the old ones. What would you say of a man covered with wounds who is advised to go to the hospital to show himself to the surgeon? The surgeon cures him by giving him remedies. But, behold! this man takes his knife, gives himself great blows with it and makes himself worse than he was before. Well, that is what you often do after leaving the confessional.

My children, some people make bad confessions without taking any notice of it. These persons

say, "I do not know what is the matter with me."
...They are tormented, and they do not know
why. They have not that agility which makes one
go straight to the good God; they have something
heavy and weary about them which fatigues them.
My children, that is because of sins that remain,
often even venial sins, for which one has some
affection. There are some people who, indeed,
tell everything, but they have no repentance; and
they go at once to Holy Communion. Thus the
Blood of Our Lord is profaned! They go to the
Holy Table with a sort of weariness. They say,
"Yet, I accused myself of all my sins...I do not
know what is the matter with me." There is an
unworthy Communion, and they were hardly
aware of it!

My children, some people again profane the
Sacraments in another manner. They have concealed mortal sins for ten years, for twenty years.
They are always uneasy; their sin is always present to their mind; they are always thinking of
confessing it, and always putting it off; it is a
Hell. When these people feel this, they will ask
to make a general confession, and they will tell
their sins as if they had just committed them:
they will not confess that they have hidden them
during ten years—twenty years. That is a bad
confession! They ought to say, besides, that they
had given up the practice of their religion, that
they no longer felt the pleasure they had formerly
in serving the good God.

My children, we run the risk again of profaning

the Sacrament if we seize the moment when there is a noise round the confessional to tell the sins quickly which give us most pain. We quiet ourselves by saying, "I accused myself properly; so much the worse if the confessor did not hear." So much the worse for you who acted cunningly! At other times we speak quickly, profiting by the moment when the priest is not very attentive to get over the great sins. Take a house which has been for a long time very dirty and neglected—it is in vain to sweep out, there will always be a nasty smell. It is the same with our soul after confession; it requires tears to purify it. My children, we must ask earnestly for repentance. After confession, we must plant a thorn in our heart, and never lose sight of our sins. We must do as the angel did to St. Francis of Assisi; he fixed in him five darts, which never came out again.

CHAPTER 18

Catechism on Suffering

WHETHER WE will or not, we must suffer. There are some who suffer like the good thief, and others like the bad thief. They both suffered equally. But one knew how to make his sufferings meritorious, he accepted them in the spirit of reparation, and turning towards Jesus crucified, he received from His mouth these beautiful words: "This day thou shalt be with Me in Paradise." The other, on the contrary, cried out, uttered imprecations and blasphemies, and expired in the most frightful despair. There are two ways of suffering—to suffer with love, and to suffer without love. The saints suffered everything with joy, patience, and perseverance, because they loved. As for us, we suffer with anger, vexation, and weariness, because we do not love. If we loved God, we should love crosses, we should wish for them, we should take pleasure in them. . . .We should be happy to be able to suffer for the love of Him who lovingly suffered for us. Of what do we complain? Alas! the poor infidels, who have not the happiness of knowing God and His infinite loveliness, have the same crosses that we have; but they have not the same consolations.

You say it is hard? No, it is easy, it is consoling, it is sweet; it is happiness. Only we must love while we suffer, and suffer while we love.

On the Way of the Cross, you see, my children, only the first step is painful. Our greatest cross is the fear of crosses. ...We have not the courage to carry our cross, and we are very much mistaken; for, whatever we do, the cross holds us tight—we cannot escape from it. What, then, have we to lose? Why not love our crosses and make use of them to take us to Heaven? But, on the contrary, most men turn their backs upon crosses, and fly before them. The more they run, the more the cross pursues them, the more it strikes and crushes them with burdens. ...If you were wise, you would go to meet it like St. Andrew, who said, when he saw the cross prepared for him and raised up into the air, "Hail O good cross! O admirable cross! O desirable cross! receive me into thine arms, withdraw me from among men, and restore me to my Master, who redeemed me through thee."

Listen attentively to this, my children: He who goes to meet the cross, goes in the opposite direction to crosses; he meets them, perhaps, but he is pleased to meet them; he loves them; he carries them courageously. They unite him to Our Lord; they purify him; they detach him from this world; they remove all obstacles from his heart; they help him to pass through life, as a bridge helps us to pass over water. ...Look at the saints; when they were not persecuted, they persecuted themselves. A good religious complained one day to Our Lord that he was persecuted. He said, "O Lord, what have I done to be treated thus?" Our Lord answered him, "And I, what had I done when I was led to Calvary?" Then the religious understood; he wept, he asked pardon, and dared not complain any more. Worldly people are miserable when they have crosses, and good Christians are miserable when they have none. The Christian lives in the midst of crosses, as the fish lives in the sea.

Look at St. Catherine; she has two crowns, that of purity and that of martyrdom: how happy she is, that dear little saint, to have chosen to suffer rather than to consent to sin! There was once a religious who loved suffering so much that he had fastened the rope from a well round his body; this cord had rubbed off the skin, and had by degrees buried itself in the flesh, out of which worms came. His brethren asked that he should be sent out of the community. He went away happy and pleased, to hide himself in a rocky cavern. But the same night the Superior heard Our Lord saying to him: "Thou hast lost the treasure of thy house." Then they went to fetch back this good saint, and they wanted to see from whence these worms came. The Superior had the cord taken off, which was done by turning back the flesh. At last he got well.

Very near this, in a neighboring parish, there was a little boy in bed, covered with sores, very ill, and very miserable; I said to him, "My poor little child, you are suffering very much!" He answered me, "No, sir; today I do not feel the pain I had yesterday, and tomorrow I shall not suffer from the pain I have now." "You would like to get well?" "No; I was naughty before I was ill, and I might be so again. I am very well as I am." We do not understand that, because we are too earthly. Children in whom the Holy Ghost dwells put us to shame.

If the good God sends us crosses, we resist, we complain, we murmur; we are so averse to whatever contradicts us, that we want to be always in a box of cotton: but we ought to be put into a box of thorns. It is by the Cross that we go to Heaven. Illnesses, temptations, troubles, are so many crosses which take us to Heaven. All this will soon be over. . . . Look at the saints, who have arrived there before us. . . . The good God does not require of us the martyrdom of the body; He requires only the martyrdom of the heart, and of the will. . . . Our Lord is our model; let us take up our cross, and follow Him. Let us do like the soldiers of Napoleon. They had to cross a bridge under the fire of grapeshot; no one dared to pass it. Napoleon took the colors, marched over first, and they all followed. Let us do the same; let us follow Our Lord, who has gone before us.

A soldier was telling me one day that during a battle he had marched for half an hour over dead bodies; there was hardly space to tread upon; the ground was all dyed with blood. Thus on the road of life we must walk over crosses and troubles

to reach our true country. The cross is the ladder
to Heaven. . . . How consoling it is to suffer under
the eyes of God, and to be able to say in the
evening, at our examination of conscience: "Come,
my soul! thou hast had today two or three hours
of resemblance to Jesus Christ. Thou hast been
scourged, crowned with thorns, crucified with
Him!" Oh what a treasure for the hour of death!
How sweet it is to die, when we have lived on
the cross! We ought to run after crosses as the
miser runs after money. . . . Nothing but crosses
will reassure us at the Day of Judgment. When
that day shall come, we shall be happy in our
misfortunes, proud of our humiliations, and rich
in our sacrifices!

If someone said to you, "I should like to become rich; what must I do?" you would answer him,
"You must labor." Well, in order to get to Heaven,
we must suffer. Our Lord shows us the way in the
person of Simon the Cyrenian; He calls His friends
to carry His Cross after Him. The good God wishes
us never to lose sight of the Cross, therefore it is
placed everywhere; by the roadside, on the heights,
in the public squares—in order that at the sight
of it we may say, "See how God has loved us!"
The Cross embraces the world; it is planted at
the four corners of the world; there is a share
of it for all. Crosses are on the road to Heaven
like a fine bridge of stone over a river, by which
to pass it. Christians who do not suffer pass this
river by a frail bridge, a bridge of wire, always
ready to give way under their feet.

He who does not love the Cross may indeed be saved, but with great difficulty: he will be a little star in the firmament. He who shall have suffered and fought for his God will shine like a beautiful sun. Crosses, transformed by the flames of love, are like a bundle of thorns thrown into the fire, and reduced by the fire to ashes. The thorns are hard, but the ashes are soft. Oh, how much sweetness do souls experience that are all for God in suffering! It is like a mixture into which one puts a great deal of oil: the vinegar remains vinegar; but the oil corrects its bitterness, and it can scarcely be perceived.

If you put fine grapes into the wine press, there will come out a delicious juice: our soul, in the wine press of the Cross, gives out a juice that nourishes and strengthens it. When we have no crosses, we are arid: if we bear them with resignation, we feel a joy, a happiness, a sweetness! . . . it is the beginning of Heaven. The good God, the Blessed Virgin, the angels, and the saints, surround us; they are by our side, and see us. The passage to the other life of the good Christian tried by affliction, is like that of a person being carried on a bed of roses. Thorns give out a perfume, and the Cross breathes forth sweetness. But we must squeeze the thorns in our hands, and press the Cross to our heart, that they may give out the juice they contain.

The Cross gave peace to the world; and it must bring peace to our hearts. All our miseries come from not loving it. The fear of crosses increases them. A cross carried simply, and without those returns of self-love which exaggerate troubles, is no longer a cross. Peaceable suffering is no longer suffering. We complain of suffering! We should have much more reason to complain of not suffering, since nothing makes us more like Our Lord than carrying His Cross. Oh, what a beautiful union of the soul with Our Lord Jesus Christ by the love and the virtue of His Cross! I do not understand how a Christian can dislike the Cross, and fly from it! Does he not at the same time fly from Him who has deigned to be fastened to it, and to die for us?

Contradictions bring us to the foot of the Cross, and the Cross to the gate of Heaven. That we may get there, we must be trodden upon, we must be set at naught, despised, crushed. . . .There are no happy people in this world but those who enjoy calmness of mind in the midst of the troubles of life: they taste the joys of the children of God. . . .All pains are sweet when we suffer in union with Our Lord. . . .To suffer! what does it signify? It is only a moment. If we could go and pass a week in Heaven, we should understand the value of this moment of suffering. We should find no cross heavy enough, no trial bitter enough. . . .The Cross is the gift that God makes to His friends.

How beautiful it is to offer ourselves every morning in sacrifice to the good God, and to accept everything in expiation of our sins! We must ask for the love of crosses; then they become sweet.

I tried it for four or five years. I was well calumniated, well contradicted, well knocked about. Oh, I had crosses indeed! I had almost more than I could carry! Then I took to asking for love of crosses, and I was happy. I said to myself, truly there is no happiness but in this! We must never think from whence crosses come: they come from God. It is always God who gives us this way of proving our love to Him.

CHAPTER 19

Catechism on Hope

M Y CHILDREN, we are going to speak of
hope: that is what makes the happiness of
man on earth. Some people in this world hope
too much, and others do not hope enough. Some
say, "I am going to commit this sin again. It will
not cost me more to confess four than three." It
is like a child saying to his father, "I am going
to give you four blows; it will cost me no more
than to give you one: I shall only have to ask
your pardon."

That is the way men behave towards the good
God. They say, "This year I shall amuse myself
again; I shall go to dances and to the alehouse,
and next year I will be converted. The good God
will be sure to receive me, when I choose to return to Him. He is not so cruel as the priests
tell us." No, the good God is not cruel, but He
is just. Do you think He will adapt Himself in
everything to your will? Do you think that He
will embrace you, after you have despised Him
all your life? Oh no, indeed! There is a certain
measure of grace and of sin after which God with-
draws Himself. What would you say of a father
who should treat a good child, and one not so

good, in the same manner? You would say: This father is not just. Well! God would not be just if He made no difference between those who serve Him and those who offend Him. My children, there is so little faith now in the world that people either hope too much, or they despair. Some say, "I have done too much evil; the good God cannot pardon me." My children, this is a great blasphemy; it is putting a limit to the mercy of God, which has no limit—it is infinite. You may have done evil enough to lose the souls of a whole parish, and if you confess, if you are sorry for having done this evil, and resolve not to do it again, the good God will have pardoned you.

A priest was once preaching on hope, and on the mercy of the good God. He reassured others, but he himself despaired. After the sermon, a young man presented himself, saying, "Father, I am come to confess to you." The priest answered, "I am willing to hear your confession." The other recounted his sins, after which he added, "Father, I have done much evil; I am lost!" "What do you say, my friend! We must never despair." The young man rose, saying, "Father, you wish me not to despair, and what do you do?" This was a ray of light; the priest, all astonishment, drove away that thought of despair, became a religious and a great saint. . . .The good God had sent him an angel under the form of a young man, to show him that we must never despair. The good God is as prompt to grant us pardon when we ask it of Him as a mother is to snatch her child out of the fire.

Chapter 20

Catechism on the Cardinal Virtues

PRUDENCE SHOWS us what is most pleasing to God, and most useful to the salvation of our soul. We must always choose the most perfect. Two good works present themselves to be done, one in favor of a person we love, the other in favor of a person who has done us some harm; well, we must give the preference to the latter. There is no merit in doing good, when a natural feeling leads us to do it. A lady, wishing to have a widow to live with her to take care of, asked St. Athanasius to find her one among the poor. Afterwards, meeting the Bishop, she reproached him that he had treated her ill, because this person was too good, and gave her nothing to do by which she could gain Heaven; and she begged him to give her another. The saint chose the worst he could find; of a cross, grumbling temper, never satisfied with what was done for her. This is the way we must act, for there is no great merit in doing good to one who values it, who thanks us and is grateful.

There are some persons who think they are never treated well enough; they seem as if they had a right to everything. They are never pleased with what is done for them: they repay everybody with ingratitude. . . . Well! those are the people to whom we should do good by preference. We must be prudent in all our actions, and seek not our own taste, but what is most pleasing to the good God. Suppose you have a franc that you intend to give for a Mass; you see a poor family in distress, in want of bread: it is better to give your money to these wretched people, because the Holy Sacrifice will still be offered; the priest will not fail to say Holy Mass; while these poor people may die of hunger. . . . You would wish to pray to the good God, to pass your whole day in the church; but you think it would be very useful to work for some poor people that you know, who are in great need; that is much more pleasing to God than your day passed before the holy tabernacle.

Temperance is another cardinal virtue: we can be temperate in the use of our imagination, by not letting it gallop as fast as it would wish; we can be temperate with our eyes, temperate with our mouth—some people constantly have something sweet and pleasant in their mouth; we can be temperate with our ears, not allowing them to listen to useless songs and conversation; temperate in smelling—some people perfume themselves to such a degree as to make those about them sick; temperate with the hands—some people are always washing them when it is hot, and handling things that are soft to the touch. . . . In short, we can practice temperance with our whole body, this poor machine, by not letting it run away like a horse without bit or bridle, but checking it and keeping it down. Some people lie buried there, in their beds; they are glad not to sleep, that they may the better feel how comfortable they are. The saints were not like that. I do not know how we are ever to get where they are. . . . Well! if we are saved, we shall stay infinitely long in Purgatory, while they will fly straight to Heaven to see the good God.

That great saint, St. Charles Borromeo, had in his apartment a fine cardinal's bed, which everybody saw; but, besides that, there was one which nobody could see, made of bundles of wood; and that was the one he made use of. He never warmed himself; when people came to see him, they remarked that he placed himself so as not to feel the fire. That is what the saints were like. They lived for Heaven, and not for earth; they were all heavenly; and as for us, we are all earthly. Oh, how I like those little mortifications that are seen by nobody, such as rising a quarter of an hour sooner, rising for a little while in the night to pray! but some people think of nothing but sleeping. There was once a solitary who had built himself a royal palace in the trunk of an oak tree; he had placed thorns inside of it, and he had fastened three stones over his head, so that when he raised himself or turned over he might feel the stones or the thorns. And we, we think of nothing but finding good beds, that we may sleep at our ease.

We may refrain from warming ourselves; if we are sitting uncomfortably, we need not try to place ourselves better; if we are walking in our garden, we may deprive ourselves of some fruit that we should like; in preparing the food, we need not eat the little bits that offer themselves; we may deprive ourselves of seeing something pretty, which attracts our eyes, especially in the streets of great towns. There is a gentleman who sometimes comes here. He wears two pairs of spectacles, that he may see nothing. ...But some heads are always in motion, some eyes are always looking about. ...When we are going along the streets, let us fix our eyes on Our Lord carrying His Cross before us; on the Blessed Virgin, who is looking at us; on our guardian angel, who is by our side. How beautiful is this interior life! It unites us with the good God. ...Therefore, when the devil sees a soul that is seeking to attain to it, he tries to turn him aside from it by filling his imagination with a thousand fancies. A good Christian does not listen to that; he goes always forward in perfection, like a fish plunging into the depths of the sea. ...As for us, alas! we drag ourselves along like a leech in the mud.

There were two saints in the desert who had sewed thorns into all their clothes; and we seek for nothing but comfort! Yet we wish to go to Heaven, but with all our luxuries, without having any annoyance; that is not the way the saints acted. They sought every way of mortifying themselves, and in the midst of all their privations they tasted infinite sweetness. How happy are those who love the good God! They do not lose a single opportunity of doing good; misers employ all the means in their power to increase their treasure; they do the same for the riches of Heaven— they are always heaping up. We shall be surprised at the Day of Judgment to see souls so rich!

— Part II —

EXPLANATIONS
AND
EXHORTATIONS

*Sixteen Exhortations of
the Holy Curé of Ars*

CHAPTER 1

On Salvation

THE HAPPINESS of man on earth, my children, is to be very good; those who are very good bless the good God, they love Him, they glorify Him, and do all their works with joy and love, because they know that we are in this world for no other end than to serve and love the good God.

Look at bad Christians; they do everything with trouble and disgust; and why, my children? because they do not love the good God, because their soul is not pure, and their hopes are no longer in Heaven, but on earth. Their heart is an impure source which poisons all their actions, and prevents them from rising to God; so they come to die without having thought of death, destitute of good works for Heaven, and loaded with crimes for Hell: this is the way they are lost forever, my children. People say it is too much trouble to save one's soul; but, my children, is it not trouble to acquire glory or fortune? Do you stay in bed when you have to go and plough, or mow, or reap? No. Well, then, why should you be more idle when you have to lay up an immense fortune which will never perish—when you have to strive for eternal glory?

See, my children, if we really wish to be saved we must determine, once for all, to labor in earnest for our salvation; our soul is like a garden in which the weeds are ever ready to choke the good plants and flowers that have been sown in it. If the gardener who has charge of this garden neglects it, if he is not continually using the spade and the hoe, the flowers and plants will soon disappear. Thus, my children, do the virtues with which God has been pleased to adorn our soul disappear under our vices if we neglect to cultivate them. As a vigilant gardener labors from morning till night to destroy the weeds in his garden, and to ornament it with flowers, so let us labor every day to extirpate the vices of our soul and to adorn it with virtues. See, my children, a gardener never lets the weeds take root, because he knows that then he would never be able to destroy them. Neither let us allow our vices to take root, or we shall not be able to conquer them.

One day, an anchorite being in a forest with a companion, showed him four cypresses to be pulled up one after the other; the young man, who did not very well know why he told him to do this, took hold of the first tree, which was quite small, and pulled it up with one hand without trouble; the second, which was a little bigger and had some roots, made him pull harder, but yet he pulled it up with one hand; the third, being still bigger, offered so much resistance, that he was obliged to take both hands and to use all his strength; the fourth, which was grown into a tree, had such deep roots, that he exhausted himself in vain efforts. The saint then said to him, "With a little vigilance and mortification, we succeed in repressing our passions, and we triumph over them when they are only springing up; but when they have taken deep root, nothing is more difficult; the thing is even impossible without a miracle."

Let us not reckon on a miracle of Providence, my children; let us not put off till the end of our life the care that we ought daily to take of our soul; let us labor while there is yet time— later it will no longer be within our power; let us lay our hands to the work; let us watch over ourselves; above all, let us pray to the good God— with His assistance we shall always have power over our passions. Man sins, my children; but if he has not in this first moment lost the faith, he runs, he hastens, he flies, to seek a remedy for his ill; he cannot soon enough find the tribunal of penance, where he can recover his happiness. That is the way we should conduct ourselves if we were good Christians. Yes, my children, we could not remain one moment under the empire of the devil; we should be ashamed of being his slaves. A good Christian watches continually, sword in hand, the the devil can do nothing against him, for he resists him like a warrior in full armor; he does not fear him, because he has rejected from his heart all that is impure. Bad Christians are idle and lazy, and stand hanging their heads; and you see how they give way at the first assault: the devil does what he pleases with them; he presents pleasures to them, he makes them taste pleasure, and then, to drown the cries of their conscience, he whispers to them in a gentle voice, "Thou wilt sin no more." And when the occasion presents itself, they fall again, and more easily than the first time. If they go to confession he makes them ashamed, they speak only in half-words, they lower their voice, they explain away their sins, and, what is more miserable, they perhaps conceal some. The good Christian, on the contrary, groans and weeps over his sins, and reaches the tribunal of Penance already half justified.

CHAPTER 2

On Death

A DAY WILL come, perhaps it is not far off, when we must bid adieu to life, adieu to the world, adieu to our relations, adieu to our friends. When shall we return, my children? Never. We appear upon this earth, we disappear, and we return no more; our poor body, that we take such care of, goes away into dust, and our soul, all trembling, goes to appear before the good God. When we quit this world, where we shall appear no more, when our last breath of life escapes, and we say our last adieu, we shall wish to have passed our life in solitude, in the depths of a desert, far from the world and its pleasures. We have these examples of repentance before our eyes every day, my children, and we remain always the same. We pass our life gaily, without ever troubling ourselves about eternity. By our indifference to the service of the good God, one would think we were never going to die.

See, my children, some people pass their whole life without thinking of death. It comes, and behold! they have nothing; faith, hope, and love, all are already dead within them. When death shall come upon us, of what use will three-quarters of our life have been to us? With what are we occupied the greatest part of our time? Are we thinking of the good God, of our salvation, of our soul? O my children! what folly is the world! We come into it, we go out of it, without knowing why. The good God places us in it to serve Him, to try if we will love Him and be faithful to His law; and after this short moment of trial, He promises us a recompense. Is it not just that He should reward the faithful servant and punish the wicked one? Should the Trappist, who has passed his life in lamenting and weeping over his sins, be treated the same as the bad Christian, who has lived in abundance in the midst of all the enjoyments of life? No; certainly not. We are on earth not to enjoy its pleasures, but to labor for our salvation.

Let us prepare ourselves for death; we have not a minute to lose: it will come upon us at the moment when we least expect it; it will take us by surprise. Look at the saints, my children, who were pure; they were always trembling, they pined away with fear; and we, who so often offend the good God—we have no fears. Life is given us that we may learn to die well, and we never think of it. We occupy ourselves with everything else. The idea of it often occurs to us, and we always reject it; we put it off to the last moment. O my children! this last moment, how much it is to be feared! Yet the good God does not wish us to despair; He shows us the good thief, touched with repentance, dying near Him on the cross; but he is the only one; and then see, he dies near the good God. Can we hope to be near Him at our last moment—we who have been far from Him all our life? What have we done to deserve that favor? A great deal of evil, and no good.

There was once a good Trappist Father, who was trembling all over at perceiving the approach of death. Someone said to him, "Father, of what then are you afraid?" "Of the judgment of God," he said. "Ah! if you dread the judgment—you who have done so much penance, you who love God so much, who have been so long preparing for death—what will become of me?" See, my children, to die well we must live well; to live well, we must seriously examine ourselves: every evening think over what we have done during the day; at the end of each week review what we have done during the week; at the end of each month review what we have done during the month; at the end of the year, what we have done during the year. By this means, my children, we cannot fail to correct ourselves, and to become fervent Christians in a short time. Then, when death comes, we are quite ready; we are happy to go to Heaven.

CHAPTER 3

On the Last Judgment

OUR CATECHISM tells us, my children, that all men will undergo a particular judgment on the day of their death. No sooner shall we have breathed our last sigh than our soul, without leaving the place where it has expired, will be presented before the tribunal of God. Wherever we may die, God is there to exercise His justice. The good God, my children, has measured out our years, and of those years that He has resolved to leave us on this earth, He has marked out one which shall be our last; one day which we shall not see succeeded by other days; one hour after which there will be for us no more time. What distance is there between that moment and this—the space of an instant. Life, my children, is a smoke, a light vapor; it disappears more quickly than a bird that darts through the air, or a ship that sails on the sea, and leaves no trace of its course!

When shall we die? Alas! will it be in a year, in a month? Perhaps tomorrow, perhaps today! May not that happen to us which happens to so many others? It may be that at a moment when you are thinking of nothing but amusing yourself, you may be summoned to the judgment of God, like the impious Baltassar. What will then be the astonishment of that soul entering on its eternity? Surprised, bewildered, separated thenceforth from its relations and friends, and, as it were, surrounded with Divine light, it will find in its Creator no longer a merciful Father, but an inflexible Judge. Imagine to yourselves, my children, a soul at its departure from this life. It is going to appear before the tribunal of its Judge, alone with God; there is Heaven on one side, Hell on the other. What object presents itself before it? The picture of its whole life! All its thoughts, all its words, all its actions, are examined.

This examination will be terrible, my children, because nothing is hidden from God. His infinite wisdom knows our most inmost thoughts; it penetrates to the bottom of our hearts, and lays open their innermost folds. In vain sinners avoid the light of day that they may sin more freely; they spare themselves a little sham in the eyes of men, but it will be of no advantage to them at the day of judgment; God will make light the darkness under cover of which they thought to sin with impunity. The Holy Ghost, my children, says that we shall be examined on our words, our thoughts, our actions; we shall be examined even on the good we ought to have done, and have not done, on the sins of others of which we have been the cause. Alas! so many thoughts to which we abandon ourselves—to which the mind gives itself up; how many in one day! in a week! in a month! in a year! How many in the whole course of our life! Not one of this infinite number will escape the knowledge of our Judge.

The proud man must give an account of all his thoughts of presumption, of vanity, of ambition; the impure of all his evil thoughts, and of the criminal desires with which he has fed his imagination. Those young people who are incessantly occupied with their dress, who are seeking to please, to distinguish themselves, to attract attention and praise, and who dare not make themselves known in the tribunal of Penance, will they be able still to hide themselves at the day of the judgment of God? No, no! They will appear there such as they have been during their life, before Him who makes known all that is most secret in the heart of man.

We shall give an account, my children, of our oaths, of our imprecations, of our curses. God hears our slanders, our calumnies, our free conversations, our worldly and licentious songs; He hears also the discourse of the impious. This is not all, my children; God will also examine our actions. He will bring to light all our unfaithfulness in His service, our forgetfulness of His Commandments, our transgression of His law, the profanation of His churches, the attachment to the world, the ill-regulated love of pleasure and of the perishable goods of earth. All, my children, will be unveiled; those thefts, that injustice, that usury, that intemperance, that anger, those disputes, that tyranny, that revenge, those criminal liberties, those abominations that cannot be named without blushes. . . .

CHAPTER 4

On Sin

*Sin is a thought, a word, an action,
contrary to the law of God.*

BY SIN, my children, we rebel against the good God, we despise His justice, we tread under foot His blessings. From being children of God, we become the executioner and assassin of our soul, the offspring of Hell, the horror of Heaven, the murderer of Jesus Christ, the capital enemy of the good God. O my children! if we thought of this, if we reflected on the injury which sin offers to the good God, we should hold it in abhorrence, we should be unable to commit it; but we never think of it, we like to live at our ease, we slumber in sin. If the good God sends us remorse, we quickly stifle it, by thinking that we have done no harm to anybody, that God is good, and that He did not place us on the earth to make us suffer.

Indeed, my children, the good God did not place us on the earth to suffer and endure, but to work out our salvation. See, He wills that we should work today and tomorrow; and after that, an eternity of joy, of happiness, awaits us in

Heaven. . . . O my children! how ungrateful we are! The good God calls us to Himself; He wishes to make us happy forever, and we are deaf to His word, we will not share His happiness; He enjoins us to love Him, and we give our heart to the devil. . . . The good God commands all nature as its Master; He makes the winds and the storms obey Him; the angels tremble at His adorable will: man alone dares to resist Him. See, God forbids us that action, that criminal pleasure, that revenge, that injustice; no matter, we are bent upon satisfying ourselves; we had rather renounce the happiness of Heaven, than deprive ourselves of a moment's pleasure, or give up a sinful habit, or change our life. What are we, then, that we dare thus to resist God? Dust and ashes, which He could annihilate with a single look. . . .

By sin, my children, we despise the good God. We renew His Death and Passion; we do as much evil as all the Jews together did, in fastening Him to the Cross. Therefore, my children, if we were to ask those who work without necessity on Sunday: "What are you doing there?" and they were to answer truly, they would say, "We are crucifying the good God." Ask the idle, the gluttonous, the immodest, what they do every day. If they answer you according to what they are really doing, they will say, "We are crucifying the good God." O my children! it is very ungrateful to offend a God who has never done us any harm; but is it not the height of ingratitude to offend a God who has done us nothing but good?

It is He who created us, who watches over us. He holds us in His hands; if He chose, He could cast us into the nothingness out of which He took us. He has given us His Son, to redeem us from the slavery of the devil; He Himself gave Him up to death that He might restore us to life; He has adopted us as His children, and ceases not to lavish His graces upon us. Notwithstanding all this, what use do we make of our mind, of our memory, of our health, of those limbs which He gave us to serve Him with? We employ them, perhaps, in committing crimes.

The good God, my children, has given us eyes to enlighten us, to see Heaven, and we use them to look at criminal and dangerous objects; He has given us a tongue to praise Him, and to express our thoughts, and we make it an instrument of iniquity—we swear, we blaspheme, we speak ill of our neighbor, we slander him; we abuse the supernatural graces, we stifle the salutary remorse by which God would convert us. . . .we reject the inspirations of our good guardian angel.

We despise good thoughts, we neglect prayer and the Sacraments. What account do we make even of the Word of God? Do we not listen to it with disgust? How miserable we are! How much we are to be pitied! We employ the time that the good God has given us for our salvation, in losing our souls. We make war upon Him with the means He has given us to serve Him; we turn His own gifts against Him! Let us cast our eyes, my children, upon Jesus fastened to the Cross, and let us say to ourselves, "This is what it has cost my Saviour to repair the injury my sins have done to God."

A God coming down to the earth to be the victim of our sins! A God suffering, a God dying, a God enduring every torment, because He has put on the semblance of sin, and has chosen to bear the weight of our iniquities! Ah, my children! at the sight of that Cross, let us conceive once for all the malice of sin, and the abhorrence in which we should hold it. . . . Let us enter into ourselves, and see what we ought to do to repair our past sins; let us implore the clemency of the good God, and let us all together say to Him, from the bottom of our heart, "O Lord, who art here crucified for us, have mercy upon us! Thou comest down from Heaven to cure souls of sin; cure us, we beseech Thee; cause our souls to be purified by approaching the tribunal of penance; yes, O God! make us look upon sin as the greatest of all evils, and by our zeal in avoiding it, and in repairing those we have had the misfortune to commit, let us one day attain to the happiness of the saints."

CHAPTER 5

On Temptations

WE ARE all inclined to sin, my children; we are idle, greedy, sensual, given to the pleasures of the flesh. We want to know everything, to learn everything, to see everything; we must watch over our mind, over our heart, and over our senses, for these are the gates by which the devil penetrates. See, he prowls round us incessantly; his only occupation in this world is to seek companions for himself. All our life he will lay snares for us, he will try to make us yield to temptations; we must, on our side, do all we can to defeat and resist him. We can do nothing by ourselves, my children; but we can do everything with the help of the good God; let us pray Him to deliver us from this enemy of our salvation, or to give strength to fight against him. With the Name of Jesus we shall overthrow the demons; we shall put them to flight. With this Name, if they sometimes dare to attack us, our battles will be victories, and our victories will be crowns for Heaven, all brilliant with precious stones.

See, my children, the good God refuses nothing to those who pray to Him from the bottom of their heart. St. Teresa, being one day in prayer, and desiring to see the good God, Jesus Christ showed to the eyes of her soul His Divine hands; then, another day, when she was again in prayer, He showed her His face. Lastly, some days after, He showed her the whole of His Sacred Humanity. The good God who granted the desire of St. Teresa will also grant our prayers. If we ask of Him the grace to resist temptations, He will grant it to us; for He wishes to save us all, He shed His Blood for us all, He died for us all, He is waiting for us all in Heaven. We are two or three hundred here: shall we all be saved, shall we all go to Heaven? Alas! my children, we know nothing about it; but I tremble when I see so many souls lost in these days.

See, they fall into Hell as the leaves fall from the trees at the approach of winter. We shall fall like the rest, my children, if we do not avoid temptations, if, when we cannot avoid them, we do not fight generously, with the help of the good God—if we do not invoke His Name during the strife, like St. Antony in the desert.

This saint having retired into an old sepulcher, the devil came to attack him; he tried at first to terrify him with a horrible noise; he even beat him so cruelly that he left him half dead and covered with wounds. "Well," said St. Antony, "here I am, ready to fight again; no, thou shalt not be able to separate me from Jesus Christ, my Lord and my God." The spirits of darkness redoubled their efforts, and uttered frightful cries. St. Antony remained unmoved, because he put all his confidence in God. After the example of this saint, my children, let us be always ready for the combat; let us put our confidence in God; let us fast and pray; and the devil will not be able to separate us from Jesus Christ, either in this world or the next.

CHAPTER 6

On Pride

*Pride is an untrue opinion of ourselves,
an untrue idea of what we are not.*

THE PROUD MAN is always disparaging himself, that people may praise him the more. The more the proud man lowers himself, the more he seeks to raise his miserable nothingness. He relates what he has done, and what he has not done; he feeds his imagination with what has been said in praise of him, and seeks by all possible means for more; he is never satisfied with praise. See, my children, if you only show some little displeasure against a man given up to self-love, he gets angry, and accuses you of ignorance or injustice towards him. . . . My children, we are in reality only what we are in the eyes of God, and nothing more. Is it not quite clear and evident that we are nothing, that we can do nothing, that we are very miserable? Can we lose sight of our sins, and cease to humble ourselves?

If we were to consider well what we are, humility would be easy to us, and the demon of pride would no longer have any room in our heart. See, *our days are like grass*—like the grass which now flourishes in the meadows, and will presently be withered; like an ear of corn which is fresh only for a moment, and is parched by the sun. In fact, my children, today we are full of life, full of health; and tomorrow, death will perhaps come to reap us and mow us down, as you reap your corn and mow your meadows. . . .Whatever appears vigorous, whatever shines, whatever is beautiful, is of short duration. . . .The glory of this world, youth, honors, riches, all pass away quickly, as quickly as the flower of grass, as the flower of the field. . . . Let us reflect that so we shall one day be reduced to dust; that we shall be thrown into the fire like dry grass, if we do not fear the good God.

Good Christians know this very well, my children; therefore they do not occupy themselves with their body; they despise the affairs of this world; they consider only their soul and how to unite it to God. Can we be proud in the face of the examples of lowliness, of humiliations, that Our Lord has given us, and is still giving us every day? Jesus Christ came upon earth, became incarnate, was born poor, lived in poverty, died on a gibbet, between two thieves. . . .He instituted an admirable Sacrament, in which He communicates Himself to us under the Eucharistic veil; and in this Sacrament He undergoes the most extraordinary humiliations. Residing continually in our tabernacles, He is deserted, misunderstood by ungrateful men; and yet He continues to love us, to serve us in the Sacrament of the Altar.

O my children! what an example of humiliation does the good Jesus give us! Behold Him on the Cross to which our sins have fastened Him; behold Him: He calls us, and says to us, "Come to Me, and learn of Me, because I am meek and humble of heart." How well the saints understood this invitation, my children! Therefore, they all sought humiliations and sufferings. After their example, then, let us not be afraid of being humbled and despised. St. John of God, at the beginning of his conversion, counterfeited madness, ran about the streets, and was followed by the populace, who threw stones at him; he always came in covered with mud and with blood. He was shut up as a madman; the most violent remedies were employed to cure him of his pretended illness; and he bore it all in the spirit of penance, and in expiation of his past sins. The good God, my children, does not require of us extraordinary things. He wills that we should be gentle, humble, and modest; then we shall always be pleasing to Him; we shall be like little children; and He will grant us the grace to come to Him and to enjoy the happiness of the saints

CHAPTER 7

On Avarice

*Avarice is an inordinate love of
the goods of this world.*

YES, MY CHILDREN, it is an ill-regulated love,
a fatal love, which makes us forget the good
God, prayer, the Sacraments, that we may love
the goods of this world—gold and silver and lands.
The avaricious man is like a pig, which seeks its
food in the mud, without caring where it comes
from. Stooping towards the earth, he thinks of
nothing but the earth; he no longer looks towards
Heaven, his happiness is no longer there. The avaricious man does no good till after his death. See,
how greedily he gathers up wealth, how anxiously
he keeps it, how afflicted he is if he loses it. In
the midst of riches, he does not enjoy them; he
is, as it were, plunged in a river, and is dying
of thirst; lying on a heap of corn, he is dying
of hunger; he has everything, my children, and
dares not touch anything; his gold is a sacred thing
to him, he makes it his divinity, he adores it. . . .

O my children! how many there are in these
days who are idolators! how many there are who
think more of making a fortune than of serving

the good God! They steal, they defraud, they go
to law with their neighbor; they do not even respect the laws of God. They work on Sundays
and holydays: nothing comes amiss to their greedy
and rapacious hands. Good Christians, my children, do not think of their body, which must end
in corruption; they think only of their soul, which
is immortal. While they are on the earth, they
occupy themselves with their soul alone. So you
see how assiduous they are at the Offices of the
Church, with what fervor they pray before the
good God, how they sanctify the Sunday, how
recollected they are at holy Mass, how happy they
are! The days, the months, the years are nothing
to them; they pass them in loving the good God,
with their eyes fixed on their eternity. . . .

Seeing us so indifferent to our salvation, and
so occupied in gathering up a little mud, would
not anyone say that we were never to die? Indeed, my children, we are like people who, during the summer, should make an ample provision
of gourds, of melons, for a long journey; after
the winter, what would remain of it? Nothing.
In the same way, my children, what remains to
the avaricious man of all his wealth when death
comes upon him unawares? A poor covering, a
few planks, and the despair of not being able to
carry his gold away with him. Misers generally
die in this sort of despair, and pay eternally to
the devil for their insatiable thirst for riches.
Misers, my children are sometimes punished even
in this world.

Once St. Hilarion, followed by a great number of his disciples, going to visit the monasteries under his rule, came to the abode of an avaricious solitary. On their approach, they found watchers in all parts of the vineyard, who threw stones and clods of earth at them to prevent their touching the grapes. This miser was well punished, for he gathered that year much fewer grapes than usual, and his wine turned into vinegar. Another solitary, named Sabbas, begged him, on the contrary, to come into his vineyard, and eat the fruit. St. Hilarion blessed it, and sent in to it his religious, to the number of three thousand, who all satisfied their hunger; and twenty days after, the vineyard yielded three hundred measures of wine, instead of the usual quantity of ten. Let us follow the example of Sabbas, and be disinterested; the good God will bless us, and after having blessed us in this world, He will also reward us in the other.

CHAPTER 8

On Lust

*Lust is the love of the pleasures that are
contrary to purity.*

NO SINS, my children, ruin and destroy a soul
so quickly as this shameful sin; it snatches
us out of the hands of the good God and hurls
us like a stone into an abyss of mire and corruption. Once plunged in this mire, we cannot get
out, we make a deeper hole in it every day, we
sink lower and lower. Then we lose the faith, we
laugh at the truths of religion, we no longer see
Heaven, we do not fear Hell. O my children! how
much are they to be pitied who give way to this
passion! How wretched they are! Their soul, which
was so beautiful, which attracted the eyes of the
good God, over which He leant as one leans over
a perfumed rose, has become like a rotten car-
cass, of which the pestilential odor rises even to
His throne. . . .

See, my children! Jesus Christ endured patiently,
among His Apostles, men who were proud, ambitious, greedy—even one who betrayed Him; but
He could not bear the least stain of impurity in
any of them; it is of all vices that which He has

most in abhorrence: "My Spirit does not dwell
in you," the Lord says, "if you are nothing but
flesh and corruption." God gives up the impure
to all the wicked inclinations of his heart. He lets
him wallow, like the vile swine, in the mire, and
does not even let him smell its offensive exhala-
tions. . . . The immodest man is odious to everyone, and is not aware of it. God has set the mark
of ignominy on his forehead, and he is not
ashamed; he has a face of brass and a heart of
bronze; it is in vain you talk to him of honor,
of virtue; he is full of arrogance and pride. The
eternal truths, death, judgment, Paradise, Hell—
nothing terrifies him, nothing can move him.

So, my children, of all sins, that of impurity
is the most difficult to eradicate. Other sins forge
for us chains of iron, but this one makes them
of bull's hide, which can be neither broken nor
rent; it is a fire, a furnace, which consumes even
to the most advanced old age. See those two infamous old men who attempted the purity of the
chaste Susannah; they had kept the fire of their
youth even till they were decrepit. When the body
is worn out with debauchery, when they can no
longer satisfy their passions, they supply the place
of it, oh, shame! by infamous desires and
memories.

With one foot in the grave, they still speak the
language of passion, till their last breath; they
die as they have lived, impenitent; for what penance can be done by the impure, what sacrifice
can be imposed on himself at his death, who

during his life has always given way to his passions? Can one at the last moment expect a good confession, a good Communion, from him who has concealed one of these shameful sins, perhaps, from his earliest youth—who has heaped sacrilege on sacrilege? Will the tongue, which has been silent up to this day, be unloosed at the last moment? No, no, my children; God has abandoned him; many sheets of lead already weigh upon him; he will add another, and it will be the last. . . .

CHAPTER 9

On Envy

Envy is a sadness which we feel on account of the good that happens to our neighbor.

ENVY, my children, follows pride; whoever is envious is proud. See, envy comes to us from Hell; the devils having sinned through pride, sinned also through envy, envying our glory, our happiness. Why do we envy the happiness and the goods of others? Because we are proud; we should like to be the sole possessors of talents, riches, of the esteem and love of all the world! We hate our equals, because they are our equals; our inferiors, from the fear that they may equal us; our superiors, because they are above us. In the same way, my children, that the devil after his fall felt, and still feels, extreme anger at seeing us the heirs of the glory of the good God, so the envious man feels sadness at seeing the spiritual and temporal prosperity of his neighbor.

We walk, my children, in the footsteps of the devil; like him, we are vexed at good, and rejoice at evil. If our neighbor loses anything, if his affairs go wrong, if he is humbled, if he is unfortunate, we are joyful...we triumph! The devil, too, is full of joy and triumph when we fall, when he can make us fall as low as himself. What does he gain by it? Nothing. Shall we be richer, because our neighbor is poorer? Shall we be greater, because he is less? Shall we be happier, because he is more unhappy? O my children! how much we are to be pitied for being like this! St. Cyprian said that other evils had limits, but that envy had none. In fact, my children, the envious man invents all sorts of wickedness; he has recourse to evil speaking, to calumny, to cunning, in order to blacken his neighbor; he repeats what he knows, and what he does not know he invents, he exaggerates. . . .

Through the envy of the devil, death entered into the world; and also through envy we kill our neighbor; by dint of malice, of falsehood, we make him lose his reputation, his place. . . . Good Christians, my children, do not do so; they envy no one; they love their neighbor; they rejoice at the good that happens to him, and they weep with him if any misfortune comes upon him. How happy should we be if we were good Christians. Ah! my children, let us, then, be good Christians and we shall no more envy the good fortune of our neighbor; we shall never speak evil of him; we shall enjoy a sweet peace; our soul will be calm, we shall find paradise on earth.

CHAPTER 10

On Gluttony

Gluttony is an inordinate love of eating and drinking.

WE ARE GLUTTONOUS, my children, when we take food in excess, more than is required for the support of our poor body; when we drink beyond what is necessary, so as even to lose our senses and our reason. . . .Oh, how shameful is this vice! How it degrades us! See, it puts us below the brutes: the animals never drink more than to satisfy their thirst: they content themselves with eating enough; and we, when we have satisfied our appetite, when our body can bear no more, we still have recourse to all sorts of little delicacies; we take wine and liquors to repletion! Is it not pitiful? We can no longer keep upon our legs; we fall, we roll into the ditch and into the mud, we become the laughing stock of everyone, even the sport of little children. . . .

If death were to surprise us in this state, my children, we should not have time to recollect ourselves; we should fall in that state into the hands of the good God. What a misfortune, my children! How would our soul be surprised! How would it be astonished! We should shudder with

horror at seeing the lost who are in Hell. . . . Do
not let us be led by our appetite; we shall ruin
our health, we shall lose our soul. . . . See, my children, intemperance and debauchery are the support of doctors; that lets them live, and gives them
a great deal of practice. . . . We hear every day,
such a one was drunk, and falling down he broke
his leg; another, passing a river on a plank, fell
into the water and was drowned. . . . Intemperance and drunkenness are the companions of the
wicked rich man. . . . A moment of pleasure in this
world will cost us very dear in the other. There
they will be tormented by a raging hunger and
a devouring thirst; they will not even have a drop
of water to refresh themselves; their tongue and
their body will be consumed by the flames for
a whole eternity. . . .

O my children! we do not think about it; and
yet that will not fail to happen to some amongst
us, perhaps even before the end of the year! St.
Paul said that those who give themselves to excess in eating and drinking shall not possess the
kingdom of God. Let us reflect on these words!
Look at the saints: they pass their life in penance, and we would pass ours in the midst of
enjoyments and pleasures. St. Elizabeth, Queen
of Portugal, fasted all Advent, and also from St.
John Baptist's day to the Assumption. Soon after,
she began another Lent, which lasted till the feast
of St. Michael. She lived upon bread and water
only on Fridays and Saturdays, and on the vigils
of the feasts of the Blessed Virgin and of the

Apostles. They say that St. Bernard drank oil for wine. St. Isidore never ate without shedding tears! If we were good Christians, we should do as the saints have done.

We should gain a great deal for Heaven at our meals; we should deprive ourselves of many little things which, without being hurtful to our body, would be very pleasing to the good God; but we choose rather to satisfy our taste than to please God; we drown, we stifle our soul in wine and food. My children, God will not say to us at the Day of Judgment, "Give Me an account of thy body"; but, "Give Me an account of thy soul; what hast thou done with it?" . . .What shall we answer Him? Do we take as much care of our soul as of our body? O my children! let us no longer live for the pleasure of eating; let us live as the saints have done; let us mortify ourselves as they were mortified. The saints never indulged themselves in the pleasures of good cheer. Their pleasure was to feed on Jesus Christ! Let us follow their footsteps on this earth, and we shall gain the crown which they have in Heaven.

CHAPTER 11

On Anger

*Anger is an emotion of the soul, which leads us
violently to repel whatever hurts or displeases us.*

THIS EMOTION, my children, comes from the
devil: it shows that we are in his hands; that
he is the master of our heart; that he holds all
the strings of it, and makes us dance as he pleases.
See, a person who puts himself in a passion is
like a puppet; he knows neither what he says,
nor what he does; the devil guides him entirely.
He strikes right and left; his hair stands up like
the bristles of a hedgehog; his eyes start out of
his head—he is a scorpion, a furious lion. . . .Why
do we, my children, put ourselves into such a
state? Is it not pitiable? It is, mind, because we
do not love the good God. Our heart is given
up to the demon of pride, who is angry when
he thinks himself despised; to the demon of avarice, who is irritated when he suffers any loss;
to the demon of luxury, who is indignant when
his pleasures are interfered with. . . .

How unhappy we are, my children, thus to be
the sport of demons? They do whatever they please
with us; they suggest to us evil-speaking, calumny,

hatred, venegeance: they even drive us so far as
to put our neighbor to death. See, Cain killed
his brother Abel out of jealousy; Saul wished to
take away the life of David; Theodosius caused
the massacre of the inhabitants of Thessalonica,
to revenge a personal affront. . . . If we do not put
our neighbor to death, we are angry with him,
we curse him, we give him to the devil, we wish
for his death, we wish for our own. In our fury,
we blaspheme the holy Name of God, we accuse
His Providence. . . . What fury, what impiety! And
what is still more deplorable, my children, we
are carried to these excesses for a trifle, for a word,
for the least injustice! Where is our faith! Where
is our reason? We say in excuse that it is anger
that makes us swear; but one sin cannot excuse
another sin. The good God equally condemns
anger, and the excesses that are its consequences. . . . How we sadden our guardian angel!
He is always there at our side to send us good
thoughts, and he sees us do nothing but evil. . . . If
we did like St. Remigius, we should never be
angry. See, this saint, being questioned by a Father of the desert how he managed to be always
in an even temper, replied, "I often consider that
my guardian angel is always by my side, who as-
sists me in all my needs, who tells me what I
ought to do and what I ought to say, and who
writes down, after each of my actions, the way
in which I have done it."

Philip II, King of Spain, having passed several
hours of the night in writing a long letter to the

Pope, gave it to his secretary to fold up and seal. He, being half asleep, made a mistake; when he meant to put sand on the letter, he took the ink bottle and covered all the paper with ink. While he was ashamed and inconsolable, the king said, quite calmly, "No very great harm is done; there is another sheet of paper"; and he took it, and employed the rest of the night in writing a second letter, without showing the least displeasure with his secretary.

CHAPTER 12

On Sloth

Sloth is a kind of cowardice and disgust, which makes us neglect and omit our duties, rather than do violence to ourselves.

ALAS, MY CHILDREN, how many slothful people there are on this earth: how many are cowardly, how many are indolent in the service of the good God! We neglect, we omit our duties of piety, just as easily as we should take a glass of wine. We will not do violence to ourselves; we will not put ourselves to any inconvenience. Everything wearies, everything disgusts the slothful man. Prayer, the holy Sacrifice of the Mass, which do so much good to pious souls, are a torture to him. He is weary and dissatisfied in church, at the foot of the altar, in the presence of the good God. At first he feels only dislike and indifference towards everything that is commanded by religion. Soon after, you can no longer speak to him either of Confession or Communion; he has no time to think of those things.

O my children! how miserable we are in losing, in this way, the time that we might so usefully employ in gaining Heaven, in preparing ourselves for eternity! How many moments are lost in doing nothing, or in doing wrong, in listening to the suggestions of the devil, in obeying him! Does not that make us tremble? If one of the lost had only a day or an hour to spend for his salvation, to what profit would he turn it! What haste he would make to save his soul, to reconcile himself with the good God! And we, my children, who have days and years to think of our salvation, to save our souls—we remain there with our arms crossed, like that man spoken of in the Gospel. We neglect, we lose our souls. When death shall come, what shall we have to present to Our Lord? Ah! my children, hear how the good God threatens the idle: "Every tree that bringeth not forth good fruit shall be cut down, and shall be cast into the fire." "Take that unprofitable servant, and cast him out into the exterior darkness, where there shall be weeping and gnashing of teeth."

Idleness is the mother of all vices. Look at the idle; they think of nothing but eating, drinking, and sleeping. They are no longer men, but stupid beasts, giving up to all their passions; they drag themselves through the mire like very swine. They are filthy, both within and without. They feed their soul only upon impure thoughts and desires. They never open their mouth but to slander their neighbor, or to speak immodest words. Their eyes, their ears, are open only to criminal objects. . . .O my children! that we may resist idleness, let us imitate the saints. Let us watch continually over ourselves; like them, let us be very zealous in fulfilling all our duties; let the devil never find us doing nothing, lest we should yield to temptation. Let us prepare ourselves for a good death, for eternity. Let us not lose our time in lukewarmness, in negligence, in our habitual infidelities. Death is advancing: tomorrow we must, perhaps, quit our relations, our friends. Let us make haste to merit the reward promised in Paradise to the faithful servant in the Gospel!

CHAPTER 13

On Grace

CAN WE, of our own strength, avoid sin, and practice virtue? No, my children, we can do nothing without the grace of God: that is an article of faith; Jesus Christ Himself taught it to us. See, the Church thinks, and all the saints have thought with her, that grace is absolutely necessary to us, and that without it we can neither believe, nor hope, nor love, nor do penance for our sins. St. Paul, whose piety was not counterfeit, assures us, on his part, that we cannot of ourselves even pronounce the name of Jesus in a manner that can gain merit for Heaven. As the earth can produce nothing unless it is fertilized by the sun, so we can do no good without the grace of the good God.

Grace, my children, is a supernatural assistance which leads us to good; for example, there is a sinner who goes into a church and hears an instruction: the preacher speaks of Hell, of the severity of the judgments of God; he feels himself interiorly urged to be converted; this interior impulse is what is called grace. See, my children, it is the good God taking that sinner by the hand, and wishing to teach him to walk. We are like little children: we do not know how to walk on the road to Heaven; we stagger, we fall, unless the hand of the good God is always ready to support us. O my children! how good is the good God! If we would think of all that He has done, of all that He still does every day for us, we should not be able to offend Him—we should love Him with all our heart; but we do not think of it, that is the reason. . . .The angels sin, and are cast into Hell. Man sins, and God promises him a Deliverer. What have we done to deserve this favor? What have we done to deserve to be born in the Catholic religion, while so many souls are every day lost in other religions? What have we done to deserve to be baptized, while so many little children in France, as well as in China and America, die without Baptism? What have we done to deserve the pardon of all the sins that we commit after the age of reason, while so many are deprived of the Sacrament of Penance?

O my children! St. Augustine says, and it is very true, that God seeks in us what deserves that He should abandon us, and finds it; and that He seeks what would make us worthy of His gifts, and finds nothing, because, in fact, there is nothing in us—we are nothing but ashes and sin. All our merit, my children, consists in cooperating with grace. See, my children, a beautiful flower has no beauty nor brilliancy without the sun; for during the night it is all withered and drooping. When the sun rises in the morning, it suddenly revives and expands. It is the same with our soul, in regard to Jesus Christ, the true Sun of justice;

it has no interior beauty but through sanctifying grace. In order to receive this grace, my children, our soul must turn to the good God by a sincere conversion: we must open our hearts to Him by an act of faith and love. As the sun alone cannot make a flower expand if it is already dead, so the grace of the good God cannot bring us back to life if we will not abandon sin.

God speaks to us, without ceasing, by His good inspirations; He sends us good thoughts, good desires. In youth, in old age, in all the misfortunes of life, He exhorts us to receive His grace, and what use do we make of His warnings? At this moment, even, are we cooperating rightly with grace? Are we not shutting the door of our heart against it? Consider that the good God will one day call you to account for what you have heard today; woe to you, if you stifle the cry that is rising from the depths of your conscience! We are in prosperity, we live in the midst of pleasures, all puffed up with pride; our heart is of ice towards the good God. It is a ball of copper, which the waters of grace cannot penetrate; it is a tree which receives the gentle dew, and bears no more fruit. . . . Let us be on our guard, my children; let us take care not to be unfaithful to grace. The good God leaves us free to choose life or death; if we choose death, we shall be cast into the fire, and we must burn forever with the devils. Let us ask pardon of God for having hitherto abused the graces He has given us, and let us humbly pray Him to grant us more.

CHAPTER 14

On Prayer

OUR CATECHISM teaches us, my children, that prayer is an elevation, an application of our mind and of our heart to God, to make known to Him our wants and to ask for His assistance. We do not see the good God, my children, but He sees us, He hears us, He wills that we should raise towards Him what is most noble in us—our mind and our heart. When we pray with attention, with humility of mind and of heart, we quit the earth, we rise to Heaven, we penetrate into the Bosom of God, we go and converse with the angels and the saints. It was by prayer that the saints reached Heaven: and by prayer we too shall reach it. Yes, my children, prayer is the source of all graces, the mother of all virtues, the efficacious and universal way by which God wills that we should come to Him.

He says to us: "Ask, and you shall receive." None but God could make such promises and keep them. See, the good God does not say to us, "Ask such and such a thing, and I will grant it;" but He says in general: "If you ask the Father anything in My name, He will give it you." O my children! ought not this promise to fill us with confidence, and to make us pray fervently all the days of our poor life? Ought we not to be ashamed of our idleness, of our indifference to prayer, when our Divine Saviour, the Dispenser of all graces, has given us such touching examples of it? For you know that the Gospel tells us He prayed often, and even passed the night in prayer? Are we as just, as holy, as this Divine Saviour? Have we no graces to ask for? Let us enter into ourselves; let us consider. Do not the continual needs of our soul and of our body warn us to have recourse to Him who alone can supply them? How many enemies to vanquish—the devil, the world, and ourselves. How many bad habits to overcome, how many passions to subdue, how many sins to efface! In so frightful and painful a situation, what remains to us, my children? The armor of the saints: prayer, that necessary virtue, indispensable to good as well as to bad Christians. . . .

Within the reach of the ignorant as well as the learned, enjoined to the simple and to the enlightened, it is the virtue of all mankind; it is the science of all the faithful! Everyone on the earth who has a heart, everyone who has the use of reason ought to love and pray to God; to have recourse to Him when He is irritated; to thank Him when He confers favors; to humble themselves when He strikes.

See, my children, we are poor people who have been taught to beg spiritually, and we do not beg. We are sick people, to whom a cure has been promised, and we do not ask for it. The good

God does not require of us fine prayers, but prayers which come from the bottom of our heart.

St. Ignatius was once travelling with several of his companions; they each carried on their shoulders a little bag, containing what was most necessary for them on the journey. A good Christian, seeing that they were fatigued, was interiorly excited to relieve them; he asked them as a favor to let him help them to carry their burdens. They yielded to his entreaties. When they had arrived at the inn, this man who had followed them, seeing that the Fathers knelt down at a little distance from each other to pray, knelt down also. When the Fathers rose again, they were astonished to see that this man had remained prostrate all the time they were praying: they expressed to him their surprise, and asked him what he had been doing. His answer edified them very much, for he said: "I did nothing but say, Those who pray so devoutly are saints: I am their beast of burden: O Lord! I have the intention of doing what they do: I say to Thee whatever they say." These were afterwards his ordinary words, and he arrived by means of this at a sublime degree of prayer. Thus, my children, you see that there is no one who cannot pray—and pray at all times, and in all places; by night or by day; amid the most severe labors, or in repose; in the country, at home, in travelling. The good God is everywhere ready to hear your prayers, provided you address them to Him with faith and humility.

CHAPTER 15

On the Love of God

"If you love Me, keep My Commandments."

NOTHING IS so common among Christians as to say, "O my God; I love Thee," and nothing more rare, perhaps, than the love of the good God. Satisfied with making outward acts of love, in which our poor heart often has no share, we think we have fulfilled the whole of the precept. An error, an illusion; for see, my children, St. John says that we must not love the good God in word, but in deed. Our Lord Jesus Christ also says, "If anyone love Me he will keep My Word." If we judge by this rule, there are very few Christians who truly love God, since there are so few who keep His Commandments. Yet nothing is more essential than the love of God. It is the first of all virtues, a virtue so necessary, that without it we shall never get to Heaven; and it is in order to love God that we are on the earth. Even if the good God did not command it, this feeling is so natural to us, that our heart should be drawn to it of its own accord.

But the misfortune is that we lavish our love upon objects unworthy of it, and refuse it to Him alone who deserves to be infinitely loved. Thus, my children, one person will love riches, another will love pleasures; and both will offer to the good God nothing but the languishing remains of a heart worn out in the service of the world. From thence comes insufficient love, divided love, which is for that very reason unworthy of the good God; for He alone, being infinitely above all created good, deserves that we should love Him above all things: more than our possessions, because they are earthly; more than our friends, because they are mortal; more than our life, because it is perishable; more than ourselves, because we belong to Him. Our love, my children, if it is true, must be without limit, and must influence our conduct. . . .

If the Saviour of the world, addressing Himself to each one of us separately, were now to ask us the same question that He formerly asked St. Peter: "Simon, son of John, lovest thou Me?" could we answer with as much confidence as that great Apostle, "Yea, Lord, Thou knowest that I love Thee"? *Domine, tu scis quia amo te.* We have perhaps pronounced these words without taking in their meaning and extent; for, my children, to love the good God is not merely to say with the mouth, "O my God! I love Thee!" Oh, no! where is the sinner who does not sometimes use this language?

To love the good God is not only to feel from time to time some emotions of tenderness towards God; this sensible devotion is not always in our own power. To love the good God is not to be faithful in fulfilling part of our duties and to neglect the rest. The good God will have no division: "Thou shalt love the Lord thy God with thy whole heart, and with thy whole soul, and with thy whole strength." This shows the strength of the Commandment to love God. To love God with our whole heart is to prefer Him to everything, so as to be ready to lose all our possessions, our honor, our life, rather than offend this good Master. To love God with our whole heart is to love nothing that is incompatible with the love of God; it is to love nothing that can share our heart with the good God: it is to renounce all our passions, all our ill-regulated desires. Is it thus, my children, that we love the good God?

To love the good God with our whole mind is to make the sacrifice to Him of our knowledge and our reason, and to believe all that He has taught. To love the good God with our whole mind is to think of Him often, and to make it our principal study to know Him well. To love the good God with our whole strength is to employ our possessions, our health, and our talents, in serving Him and glorifying Him. It is to refer all our actions to Him, as our last end. Once more, is it thus that we love the good God? Judging by this invariable rule, how few Christians truly love God!

Do those bad Christians love the good God, who are the slaves of their passions? Do those worldly persons love the good God, who seek only to gratify their body and to please the world? Is God loved by the miser, who sacrifices Him for a vile gain? Is He loved by that voluptuary, who abandons himself to vices the most opposite to divine love? Is He loved by that man who thinks of nothing but wine and good cheer? Is He loved by that other man, who cherishes an aversion to his neighbor, and will not forgive him? Is He loved by that young girl, who loves nothing but pleasures, and thinks of nothing but indulgence and vanity? No, no, my children, none of these persons love the good God; for we must love Him with a love of preference, with an active love!

If we had rather offend the good God than deprive ourselves of a passing satisfaction, than renounce those guilty meetings, those shameful passions, we do not love the good God with a love of preference, since we love our pleasures, our passions, better than the good God Himself. Let us go down into our own souls; let us question our hearts, my children, and see if we do not love some creature more than the good God. We are permitted to love our relations, our possessions, our health, our reputation; but this love must be subordinate to the love we should have for God, so that we may be ready to make the sacrifice of it if He should require it. . . .

Can you suppose that you are in these dispositions—you who look upon mortal sin as a trifle, who keep it quietly on your conscience for months, for years, though you know that you are in a state most displeasing to the good God? Can you suppose that you love the good God? Can you suppose that you love the good God—you who make no efforts to correct yourselves; you who will deprive yourselves of nothing; you who offend the Creator every time that you find opportunity? Yes, my children, what the miser loves with his whole heart is money; what the drunkard loves with his whole heart is wine; what the libertine loves with his whole heart is the object of his passion. You, young girls, you who had rather offend God than give up your finery and your vanities, you say that you love God; say rather that you love yourselves.

No, no, my children; it is not thus that the good God is to be loved, for we must love Him not only with a love of preference, but also with an active love. "Love," says St. Augustine, "cannot remain without the constant action of the soul: *Non potest vacare amor in anima amantis.* Yes," says this great saint, "seek for a love that does not manifest itself in works, and you will find none." What! could it be, O my God, that Thy love alone should be barren, and that the Divine fire, which ought to enkindle the whole world, should be without activity and without strength?

When you love a person, you show him the more or less affection according as the ardor of your love for him is more or less great. See, my children, what the saints were like, who were all filled with the love of the good God: nothing cost them too much; they joyfully made the greatest sacrifices; they distributed their goods to the poor, rendered services to their enemies, led a hard and penitential life; tore themselves from the pleasures of the world, from the conveniences of life, to bury themselves alive in solitude; they hastened to torments and to death, as people hasten to a feast. Such were the effects which the love of the good God produced in the saints; such ought it to produce in us. But, my children, we are not penetrated with the love of God; we do not love the good God. Can anyone say, indeed, that he loves the good God, who is so easily frightened, and who is repulsed by the least difficulty? Alas! what would have become of us if Jesus Christ had loved us only as we love Him? But, no. Triumphing over the agonies of the Cross, the bitterness of death, the shame of the most ignominious tortures, nothing costs Him too dear when He has to prove that He loves us. That is our only model. If our love is active, it will manifest itself by the works which are the effects of love, because the love of the good God is not only a love of preference, but a pious affection, a love of obedience, which makes us practice His Commandments; an active love, which makes us fulfill all the duties of a good Christian. Such is the love, my children, which God requires from us, to which He has so many titles, which He has purchased by so many benefits heaped upon us by His death for us upon the Cross. What happiness, my children, to love the good God! There is no joy, no happiness, no peace, in the heart of those who do not love the good God on earth. We desire Heaven, we aspire to it; but, that we may be sure to attain to it, let us begin to love the good God here below, in order to be able to love Him, to possess Him eternally in His holy Paradise.

CHAPTER 16

On Paradise

"Blessed, O Lord, are those who dwell in Thy house: they shall praise Thee for ever and ever."

TO DWELL in the house of the good God, to enjoy the presence of the good God, to be happy with the happiness of the good God—oh, what happiness, my children! Who can understand all the joy and consolation with which the saints are inebriated in Paradise? St. Paul, who was taken up into the third heaven, tells us that there are things above which he cannot reveal to us, and which we cannot comprehend. . . . Indeed, my children, we can never form a true idea of Heaven till we shall be there. It is a hidden treasure, an abundance of secret sweetnesses, a plenitude of joy, which may be felt, but which our poor tongue cannot explain. What can we imagine greater? The good God Himself will be our recompense: *Ego merces tua magna nimis—I am thy reward exceeding great.* O God! the happiness Thou promisest us is such that the eyes of man cannot see it, his ears cannot hear it, nor his heart conceive it.

Yes, my children, the happiness of Heaven is

incomprehensible; it is the last effort of the good God, who wishes to reward us. God, being admirable in all His works, will be so too when He recompenses the good Christians who have made all their happiness consist in the possession of Heaven. This possession contains all good, and excludes all evil; sin being far from Heaven, all the pains and miseries which are the consequences of sin are also banished from it. No more death! The good God will be in us the Principle of everlasting life. No more sickness, no more sadness, no more pains, no more grief. You who are afflicted, rejoice! Your fears and your weeping will not extend beyond the grave. . . . The good God will Himself wipe away your tears! Rejoice, O you whom the world persecutes! your sorrows will soon be over, and for a moment of tribulation, you will have in Heaven an immense weight of glory. Rejoice! for you possess all good things in one— the source of all good, the good God Himself.

Can anyone be unhappy when he is with the good God; when he is happy with the happiness of the good God, of the good God Himself; when he sees the good God as he sees himself? As St. Paul says, my children, we shall see God face to face, because then there will be no veil between Him and us. We shall possess Him without uneasiness, for we shall no longer fear to lose Him. We shall love Him with an uninterrupted and undivided love, because He alone will occupy our whole heart. We shall enjoy Him without weariness, because we shall discover in Him ever new perfections; and in proportion as we penetrate into that immense abyss of wisdom, of goodness, of mercy, of justice, of grandeur, and of holiness, we shall plunge ourselves in it with fresh eagerness. If an interior consolation, if a grace from the good God, gives us so much pleasure in this world that it diminishes our troubles, that it helps us to bear our crosses, that it gives to so many martyrs strength to suffer the most cruel torments —what will be the happiness of Heaven, where consolations and delights are given, not drop by drop, but by torrents!

Let us represent to ourselves, my children, an everlasting day always new, a day always serene, always calm; the most delicious, the most perfect society. What joy, what happiness, if we could possess on earth, only for a few minutes, the angels, the Blessed Virgin, Jesus Christ! In Heaven we shall eternally see, not only the Blessed Virgin and Jesus Christ, we shall see the good God Himself! We shall see Him no longer through the darkness of faith, but in the light of day, in all His Majesty! What happiness thus to see the good God! The angels have contemplated Him since the beginning of the world, and they are not satiated; it would be the greatest misfortune to them to be deprived of Him for a single moment. The possession of Heaven, my children, can never weary us; we possess the good God, the Author of all perfections. See, the more we possess God, the more He pleases; the more we know Him, the more attractions and charms we find in the knowledge of Him. We shall always see Him and shall always desire to see Him; we shall always taste the pleasure there is in enjoying the good God, and we shall never be satiated with it. The blessed will be enveloped in the Divine Immensity, they will revel in delights and be all surrounded with them, and, as it were, inebriated. Such is the happiness which the good God destines for us.

We can all, my children, acquire this happiness. The good God wills the salvation of the whole world; He has merited Heaven for us by His death, and by the effusion of all His Blood. What a happiness to be able to say, "Jesus Christ died for me; He has opened Heaven for me; it is my inheritance. . . . Jesus has prepared a place for me; it only depends on me to go and occupy it. *Vado vobis parare locum—I go to prepare a place for you.* The good God has given us faith, and with this virtue we can attain to eternal life. For, though the good God wills the salvation of all men, He particularly wills that of the Christians who believe in Him: *Qui credit, habeat vitam aeternam—He that believeth hath life everlasting.* Let us, then, thank the good God, my children; let us rejoice—our names are written in Heaven, like those of the Apostles. Yes, they are written in the Book of Life: if we choose, they will be there forever, since we have the means of reaching Heaven.

The happiness of Heaven, my children, is easy to acquire; the good God has furnished us with so many means of doing it! See, there is not a single creature which does not furnish us with the means of attaining to the good God; if any of them become an obstacle, it is only by our abuse of them. The goods and the miseries of this life, even the chastisements made use of by the good God to punish our infidelities, serve to our salvation. The good God, as St. Paul says, makes all things turn to the good of His elect; even our very faults may be useful to us; even bad examples and temptations. Job was saved in the midst of an idolatrous people. All the saints have been tempted. If these things are, in the hands of God, an assistance in reaching Heaven, what will happen if we have recourse to the Sacraments, to that never-failing source of all good, to that fountain of grace supplied by the good God Himself! It was easy for the disciples of Jesus to be saved, having the Divine Saviour constantly with them. Is it more difficult for us to secure our salvation, having Him constantly with us? They were happy in obtaining whatever they wished for, whatever they chose; are we less so? We possess Jesus Christ in the Eucharist; He is continually with us, He is ready to grant us whatever we ask, He is waiting for us; we have only to ask. O my children! the poor know how to express their wants to the rich; we have only our indifference, then, to accuse, if assistance and graces are wanting to us. If an ambitious or a covetous man had as ample means of enriching himself, would he hesitate a moment, would he let so favorable an opportunity escape? Alas! we do everything for this world, and nothing for the other? What labor, what trouble, what cares, what sorrows, in order to gather up a little fortune! See, my children, of what use are our perishable goods? Solomon, the greatest, the richest, the most fortunate of kings, said, in the height of the most brilliant fortune: "I have seen all things that are done under the sun; and behold, all is vanity and vexation of spirit."

And these are the goods to acquire which we labor so much, whilst we never think of the goods of Heaven! How shameful for us not to labor to acquire it, and to neglect so many means of reaching it! If the fig tree was cast into the fire for not having profited by the care that had been taken to render it fertile; if the unprofitable servant was reproved for having hidden the talent that he had received, what fate awaits us, who have so often abused the aids which might have taken us to Heaven? If we have abused the graces that the good God has given us, let us make haste to repair the past by great fidelity, and let us endeavor to acquire merits worthy of eternal life.

If you have enjoyed this book, consider making your next selection from among the following . . .

Prices guaranteed through December 31, 1995.

Miraculous Images of Our Lady. *Joan Carroll Cruz* 20.00
Brief Catechism for Adults. *Fr. Cogan* 9.00
Raised from the Dead. *Fr. Hebert* 15.00
Autobiography of St. Margaret Mary 4.00
Thoughts and Sayings of St. Margaret Mary 3.00
The Voice of the Saints. *Comp. by Francis Johnston* 5.00
The 12 Steps to Holiness and Salvation. *St. Alphonsus* . . 7.00
The Rosary and the Crisis of Faith. *Cirrincione/Nelson* . . 1.25
Sin and Its Consequences. *Cardinal Manning* 5.00
Fourfold Sovereignty of God. *Cardinal Manning* 5.00
Dialogue of St. Catherine of Siena. *Transl. Thorold* 9.00
Catholic Answer to Jehovah's Witnesses. *D'Angelo* 8.00
Twelve Promises of the Sacred Heart. (100 cards) 5.00
St. Aloysius Gonzaga. *Fr. Meschler* 10.00
The Love of Mary. *D. Roberto* 7.00
Begone Satan. *Fr. Vogl* 2.00
The Prophets and Our Times. *Fr. R. G. Culleton* 11.00
St. Therese, The Little Flower. *John Beevers* 4.50
Mary, The Second Eve. *Cardinal Newman* 2.50
Devotion to Infant Jesus of Prague. Booklet 75
The Wonder of Guadalupe. *Francis Johnston* 6.00
Apologetics. *Msgr. Paul Glenn* 9.00
Baltimore Catechism No. 1 . . . . 3.00
Baltimore Catechism No. 2 . . . . 4.00
Baltimore Catechism No. 3 . . . . 7.00
An Explanation of the Baltimore Catechism. *Kinkead* . . . 13.00
Bible History. *Schuster* 10.00
Blessed Eucharist. *Fr. Mueller* 9.00
Catholic Catechism. *Fr. Faerber* 5.00
The Devil. *Fr. Delaporte* 5.00
Dogmatic Theology for the Laity. *Fr. Premm* 18.00
Evidence of Satan in the Modern World. *Cristiani* 8.50
Fifteen Promises of Mary. (100 cards) 5.00
Life of Anne Catherine Emmerich. 2 vols. *Schmoger* 37.50
Life of the Blessed Virgin Mary. *Emmerich* 15.00
Prayer to St. Michael. (100 leaflets) 5.00
Prayerbook of Favorite Litanies. *Fr. Hebert* 9.00
Preparation for Death. (Abridged). *St. Alphonsus* 7.00
Purgatory Explained. *Schouppe* 13.50
Purgatory Explained. (pocket, unabr.). *Schouppe* 9.00
Spiritual Conferences. *Tauler* 12.00
Trustful Surrender to Divine Providence. *Bl. Claude* 4.00
Wife, Mother and Mystic. *Bessieres* 7.00
The Agony of Jesus. *Padre Pio* 1.50

Prices guaranteed through December 31, 1995.

Catholic Home Schooling. *Mary Kay Clark*............15.00
The Cath. Religion—Illus. & Expl. *Msgr. Burbach*..... 9.00
Wonders of the Holy Name. *Fr. O'Sullivan*........... 1.50
How Christ Said the First Mass. *Fr. Meagher*........16.50
Too Busy for God? Think Again! *D'Angelo*........... 4.00
St. Bernadette Soubirous. *Trochu*..................16.50
Passion and Death of Jesus Christ. *Liguori*........... 8.50
Treatise on the Love of God. 2 Vols. *de Sales*........16.50
Confession Quizzes. Radio Replies Press.............. 1.00
St. Philip Neri. *Fr. V. J. Matthews*................ 4.50
St. Louise de Marillac. *Sr. Vincent Regnault*........... 4.50
The Old World and America. *Rev. Philip Furlong*.....16.50
Prophecy for Today. *Edward Connor*................ 4.50
Bethlehem. *Fr. Faber*..........................16.50
The Book of Infinite Love. *Mother de la Touche*..... 4.50
The Church Teaches. Church Documents.............15.00
Conversation with Christ. *Peter T. Rohrbach*........... 8.00
Purgatory and Heaven. *J. P. Arendzen*............. 3.50
Liberalism Is a Sin. *Sarda y Salvany*................ 6.00
Spiritual Legacy/Sr. Mary of Trinity. *van den Broek*..... 9.00
The Creator and the Creature. *Fr. Frederick Faber*.....13.50
Radio Replies. 3 Vols. Frs. *Rumble and Carty*........36.00
Convert's Catechism of Catholic Doctrine. *Geiermann*... 3.00
Incarnation, Birth, Infancy of Jesus Christ. *Liguori* 8.50
Light and Peace. *Fr. R. P. Quadrupani*............. 5.00
Dogmatic Canons & Decrees of Trent, Vat. I.......... 8.00
The Evolution Hoax Exposed. *A. N. Field*............ 6.00
The Priest, the Man of God. *St. Joseph Cafasso*.......12.00
Christ Denied. *Fr. Paul Wickens*.................. 2.00
New Regulations on Indulgences. *Fr. Winfrid Herbst*.... 2.50
A Tour of the Summa. *Msgr. Paul Glenn*............18.00
Spiritual Conferences. *Fr. Frederick Faber*............13.50
Bible Quizzes. Radio Replies Press.................. 1.00
Marriage Quizzes. Radio Replies Press............... 1.00
True Church Quizzes. Radio Replies Press............. 1.00
St. Lydwine of Schiedam. *J. K. Huysmans*............ 7.00
Mary, Mother of the Church. Church Documents....... 3.00
The Sacred Heart and the Priesthood. *de la Touche*..... 7.00
Blessed Sacrament. *Fr. Faber*....................16.50
Revelations of St. Bridget. *St. Bridget of Sweden*....... 2.50
Magnificent Prayers. *St. Bridget of Sweden*........... 1.50
The Happiness of Heaven. *Fr. J. Boudreau*........... 7.00
The Glories of Mary. *St. Alphonsus Liguori*..........16.50
The Glories of Mary. (pocket, unabr.). *St. Alphonsus* ... 9.00

Prices guaranteed through December 31, 1995.

Eucharistic Miracles. *Joan Carroll Cruz* 13.00
The Curé D'Ars. *Abbé Francis Trochu* 20.00
Humility of Heart. *Fr. Cajetan da Bergamo* 7.00
Love, Peace and Joy. (St. Gertrude). *Prévot* 5.00
Père Lamy. *Biver* 10.00
Passion of Jesus & Its Hidden Meaning. *Groenings* 12.50
Mother of God & Her Glorious Feasts. *Fr. O'Laverty* . . . 9.00
Song of Songs—A Mystical Exposition. *Fr. Arintero* 18.00
Love and Service of God, Infinite Love. *de la Touche* . . .10.00
Life & Work of Mother Louise Marg. *Fr. O'Connell* 10.00
Martyrs of the Coliseum. *O'Reilly* 16.50
Rhine Flows into the Tiber. *Fr. Wiltgen* 13.00
What Catholics Believe. *Fr. Lawrence Lovasik* 4.00
Who Is Teresa Neumann? *Fr. Charles Carty* 2.00
Summa of the Christian Life. 3 Vols. *Granada* 36.00
St. Francis of Paola. *Simi and Segreti* 7.00
The Rosary in Action. *John Johnson* 8.00
St. Dominic. *Sr. Mary Jean Dorcy* 8.00
Is It a Saint's Name? *Fr. William Dunne* 1.50
St. Martin de Porres. *Giuliana Cavallini* 11.00
Douay-Rheims New Testament. Paperbound 13.00
St. Catherine of Siena. *Alice Curtayne* 12.00
Blessed Virgin Mary. *Liguori* 4.50
Chats with Converts. *Fr. M. D. Forrest* 9.00
The Stigmata and Modern Science. *Fr. Charles Carty* . . . 1.25
St. Gertrude the Great 1.25
Thirty Favorite Novenas 75
Brief Life of Christ. *Fr. Rumble* 2.00
Catechism of Mental Prayer. *Msgr. Simler* 1.50
On Freemasonry. *Pope Leo XIII* 1.25
Thoughts of the Curé D'Ars. *St. John Vianney* 1.50
Incredible Creed of Jehovah Witnesses. *Fr. Rumble* 1.00
St. Pius V—His Life, Times, Miracles. *Anderson* 4.00
St. Dominic's Family. *Sr. Mary Jean Dorcy* 24.00
St. Rose of Lima. *Sr. Alphonsus* 12.50
Latin Grammar. *Scanlon & Scanlon* 13.50
Second Latin. *Scanlon & Scanlon* 12.00
St. Joseph of Copertino. *Pastrovicchi* 4.50
Three Ways of the Spiritual Life. *Garrigou-Lagrange* 4.00
Mystical Evolution. 2 Vols. *Fr. Arintero, O.P.* 30.00
My God, I Love Thee. (100 cards) 5.00
St. Catherine Labouré of the Mirac. Medal. *Fr. Dirvin* . .12.50
Manual of Practical Devotion to St. Joseph. *Patrignani* . .13.50
The Active Catholic. *Fr. Palau* 6.00

Prices guaranteed through December 31, 1995.

Ven. Jacinta Marto of Fatima. *Cirrincione* 1.50
Reign of Christ the King. *Davies* 1.25
St. Teresa of Ávila. *William Thomas Walsh* 18.00
Isabella of Spain—The Last Crusader. *Wm. T. Walsh* 20.00
Characters of the Inquisition. *Wm. T. Walsh* 12.50
Philip II. *William Thomas Walsh.* H.B. 37.50
Blood-Drenched Altars—Cath. Comment. Hist. Mexico. . 18.00
Self-Abandonment to Divine Providence. *de Caussade* . . . 16.50
Way of the Cross. *Liguorian* 75
Way of the Cross. *Franciscan* 75
Modern Saints—Their Lives & Faces, Bk. 1. *Ann Ball* . . . 18.00
Modern Saints—Their Lives & Faces, Bk. 2. *Ann Ball* . . 20.00
Saint Michael and the Angels. *Approved Sources* 5.50
Dolorous Passion of Our Lord. *Anne C. Emmerich* 15.00
Our Lady of Fatima's Peace Plan from Heaven. Booklet . .75
Divine Favors Granted to St. Joseph. *Pere Binet* 4.00
St. Joseph Cafasso—Priest of the Gallows. *St. J. Bosco* . . 3.00
Catechism of the Council of Trent. *McHugh/Callan* 20.00
Padre Pio—The Stigmatist. *Fr. Charles Carty* 13.50
Why Squander Illness? *Frs. Rumble & Carty* 2.00
Fatima—The Great Sign. *Francis Johnston* 7.00
Heliotropium—Conformity of Human Will to Divine 11.00
Charity for the Suffering Souls. *Fr. John Nageleisen* 15.00
Devotion to the Sacred Heart of Jesus. *Verheylezoon* 13.00
Sermons on Prayer. *St. Francis de Sales* 3.50
Sermons on Our Lady. *St. Francis de Sales* 9.00
Sermons for Lent. *St. Francis de Sales* 10.00
Fundamentals of Catholic Dogma. *Ott* 20.00
Litany of the Blessed Virgin Mary. (100 cards) 5.00
Who Is Padre Pio? Radio Replies Press 1.50
Child's Bible History. *Knecht* 4.00
The Life of Christ. 4 Vols. H.B. *Anne C. Emmerich* 55.00
St. Anthony—The Wonder Worker of Padua. *Stoddard* . . . 4.00
The Precious Blood. *Fr. Faber* 11.00
The Holy Shroud & Four Visions. *Fr. O'Connell* 2.00
Clean Love in Courtship. *Fr. Lawrence Lovasik* 2.50
The Secret of the Rosary. *St. Louis De Montfort* 3.00
The History of Antichrist. *Rev. P. Huchede* 3.00
Where We Got the Bible. *Fr. Henry Graham* 5.00
Hidden Treasure—Holy Mass. *St. Leonard* 4.00
Imitation of the Sacred Heart of Jesus. *Fr. Arnoudt* 13.50
The Life & Glories of St. Joseph. *Edward Thompson* . . . 13.50

At your bookdealer or direct from the publisher.

Prices guaranteed through December 31, 1995.

GIVE COPIES OF THIS BOOK...

To friends and relatives, to priests and bishops, to nuns and religious, to members of your parish and religious group, to high school and college students, to the religiously committed and the fallen-away, to Catholics and non-Catholics, to teachers and educators, to molders of public opinion and political leaders, to doctors and lawyers, to Protestants and Jews, to atheists and agnostics—in short, you can give this book to anyone. The issue is the salvation of souls. For probably no other Catholic writer, no other priest, no other saint has ever written with such persuasion as Saint John Vianney, the Curé of Ars. His words touch a sympathetic chord in every Catholic heart. His words reduce the Christian message to its simplest terms—which can be understood by all. For what do we sell our immortal souls, he asks, but for "the smoke of this world." With three simple words he sums up all the sinful vanity to which humankind is attached.

This and similar expressions give his entreaties such cogency. It might safely be said that not even the Bible is written with a more impassioned appeal to souls to renounce sin and to turn to God. Constantly, he urges us to turn to Christ through His Church and through the Sacraments He has instituted to help poor sinners unburden their souls and strengthen themselves with His grace. St. John Vianney shows us all the snares and traps of the devil which lie before us, waiting to catch us in their power. But he also constantly points out the saving grace of the Sacraments to help us keep from sin—or to pluck us from its clutches if we should be so unfortunate as to fall into it.

The Little Catechism of the Curé of Ars is a book destined to do great good for the welfare of souls. It is a book you can give to your friends and relatives, to young people and old, and know that it will not offend, for its author is the heart and soul of love, and the love of God and of neighbor breathe through its every sentence and word.

This popular edition of *The Little Catechism of the Curé of Ars* has been modestly priced and generously discounted to help you purchase the book in quantity and pass it out to your friends and relatives. In doing this, you will be extending the influence and the appeal of one of Christ's greatest saints, and in effect you will be promoting the essential message of the very Gospels themselves. Also, you will be partaking in that apostolic effort Our Lord enjoined when He commissioned the Apostles: "Going therefore, teach ye all nations. . .teaching them to observe all things whatsoever I have commanded you." (*Matt.* 28: 19-20).

Quantity Discount

1 copy	4.00	
5 copies	3.00 each	15.00 total
10 copies	2.50 each	25.00 total
15 copies	2.25 each	33.75 total
25 copies	2.00 each	50.00 total
50 copies	1.75 each	87.50 total
100 copies	1.50 each	150.00 total
500 copies	1.25 each	625.00 total

Priced low purposely for wide distribution.

————— **Cut Out and Mail** —————

ORDER FORM

TAN BOOKS AND PUBLISHERS, INC.
P.O. Box 424
Rockford, Illinois 61105

Gentlemen:

Please send me _____ copies of **The Little Cate-chism of the Curé of Ars.** Enclosed is my payment in the amount of _____ .

Name _____

Street _____

City _____

State _____ Zip _____

Alternate Payment Plan

Please charge to my _____ VISA _____ MasterCard.

My Account No. is _____

4-Digit No. on MasterCard only _____

My card expires (give mo. and Yr.) _____

Signature _____